Raising Black Boys

by Dr. Jawanza Kunjufu

Chicago, Illinois

First Edition, Second Printing

Front cover illustration by Harold Carr, Jr.

Copyright © 2007 by Jawanza Kunjufu

Printed in the United States of America

10-Digit ISBN #: 1-934155-07-3
13-Digit ISBN #: 978-1-934155-07-1
Library of Congress: 2007904845

Contents

Dedication

I'm dedicating this book to my father, Eddie Brown, and my mother, Mary Brown, both of whom have gone on to be with the Lord. I want to thank them for raising me and making my life their priority. Throughout this book, my prayer is that parents will realize that childrearing must be their number one priority. It was definitely my parents' priority.

I dedicate this book to my two sons, Walker and Shik. They have grown up to be fine young men. They are responsible, they have a good work ethic, and they value family.

I dedicate this book to my only grandson, Phoenix (I'm sure more will come). I pray his parents will continue to raise him to be all that God wants him to be.

I dedicate this book to my late mentor, Val Jordan, who died at the young age of 86. He invested a lot of time in me. This elder took the role of being my mentor seriously. I ask all men who are over 40 years old: Who are you mentoring? Do you take that role seriously?

Saving the best for last, I'd like to dedicate this book to my best friend, my wife, and business partner, Rita. Beside, not behind or in front, every good man is a good woman. I've been blessed to have the best.

Preface

Parents and guardians of boys, as you read this book, keep in mind the one major indicator of your son's overall well being: his **spirit**. Too many of our boys are suffering from broken spirits. During the preschool and kindergarten years, our boys are energetic and curious, they love learning and ask thousands of questions, and there's a glow in their eyes. For your son's sake, always make sure the glow remains in his eyes. **Don't let school or any institution or any person break your son's spirit.** It is impossible to reach your full potential if your spirit has been broken—if you are no longer curious, if you no longer possess enthusiasm, if your eyes have grown dim.

I also want you to keep in mind that the three greatest influences on your son are peer pressure, rap music, and television. You must do everything within your power to monitor your son's friends, his music, and favorite television programs.

Chapter 1: Framework

Fathers know when it's time for sons
to leave home. Mothers know the time
for their daughters.

Why does parent involvement in school
decline as the child grows older?

What is the difference between a male, a boy,
and a man?

Are you raising a sperm donor or a daddy?

Are you raising a scholar or a thug?

Are you raising an honor roll student or
a class clown?

Are girls smarter than boys?

Are girls more responsible than boys?

Are girls more focused and organized than boys?

Your son's primary job is to be a student.

The future of the Black race lies in the hands of White female teachers and single-parent mothers.

Show me your son's friends, and I will show you his future.

Many boys believe their four best career options are the NBA, NFL, being a rapper, or becoming the first drug dealer never to be caught.

The greatest gift you can give your son
is to introduce him to Jesus.

There's a rumor that in Asian and Jewish
homes, any grade less than an A means that
changes will have to be made. In White
homes, anything less than a B means that
changes will be made. Unfortunately,
in Black homes, as long as you pass,
everything is okay.

What are your expectations of your son?

How long can your son stay in your house?

Boys who lack goals, make silly mistakes.

Mothers who act like girlfriends nag and
negotiate with their sons.

Parenting is a 24/7 job that lasts a minimum of 18 years. If you don't parent correctly, your son may be with you for the rest of your life.

The teacher has your son for 180 days. You have your son for a minimum of 18 years.

Is there a connection between the schoolhouse track and the jailhouse track?

You must be very careful with the large, insecure male ego.

Do not let anyone break your son's spirit.

Why are boys bored with school?

Do female teachers design a female classroom for male students?

Every boy needs a male role model. You
can't be what you have not seen.
Boys will be what they see.

Boys love video games because
losses are private.

Males compete in areas where they
believe they have a chance of winning.

Items in scholars' homes are different
from those in the homes of thugs, clowns,
pimps, and ball players.

Do you have more books than CDs
in your house?

The car note should never exceed
the rent or mortgage.

It is not the size or gender of the parent but his or her self-respect.

The quality of your conversation is a critical aspect of raising your son.

Do your son's friends know him better than you do?

Governors determine prison growth based on fourth grade reading scores.

There are two critical times when boys will challenge you: ages 2 and 12.
You must be ready for the challenges
or they will never respect you.

Is your son suffering from ADD
(Attention Deficit Disorder) or DDD
(Dad Deficiency Disorder)?

Dads, whatever happens in your marriage,
don't divorce your kids.

If you want your son to stay with you forever,
don't make him do chores, and don't teach
him how to run a household.

Many fatherless boys are aggressive and
possess a derogatory attitude toward females.

Is marriage only for White people?
Is shacking primarily for Black people?

Do mothers have 25,000 words to share with
their sons, and fathers less than 10,000?

Is it wrong for Don Imus and other Whites
to use the N, H, and B words
but okay for your son to use them?

A sperm donor who only stays for 18 seconds has no right to call himself a father. A (step)father who stays forever should not be denied the right of calling himself a father.

In the past, children were raised by parents. Today many are reared by live-in boyfriends, girlfriends, and indefinite fiancés.

Is the village strong enough to raise its boys given the fact that 68 percent of them lack fathers in the home?

Why do some parents give their sons a choice between playing basketball or attending a mentoring program; hanging out or being tutored; playing video games or attending a rites of passage program?

This may be the first generation of Black boys
to never leave home.

The chances of a lukewarm Christian parent
developing a son on fire for the Lord
are remote.

The best classroom is your living room.
A son will treat his wife or significant other
based on what he saw at home.

Parents must have higher goals and expectations for their sons than just avoiding jail.

Your son is not your property to be
withheld from his father because you want to
hurt your ex.

Fathers, you are the most important
role models in your sons' lives.

Mothers, do you see your son as a
future husband and father?

The future of your son will be determined by
how much idle time you allow him to have.

The problem is not with our boys but with
parents who lack self-esteem and a plan to
raise them.

Adult males who are unemployed or can't
keep a job were not required as boys to get
up early and do chores well.

Boys measure everything they do or say by
one yardstick: does this make me look weak?

When a grown man cries in therapy, it is
almost always about his father.

Around the age of 12, a boy picks a man to
admire and imitates him for the rest of his life.

Do we have more male homosexuals
because not all males want to be hard,
thuggish, and athletic?

Does the Black male peer group reject males
who make the honor roll, are active in the
science fair, sing in the choir,
and hate sports?

Your son's diet will dictate whether he dies
of heart disease, cancer, or diabetes.

Is there a relationship between a mama's boy
and a shacker?

Is there a relationship between a mama's boy
and a pimp?

Is television raising our boys to be homosexuals?

Is gangsta rap raising our boys to
disrespect women?

The average father only spends seven
minutes a day talking to his children.
The average mother only spends 34 minutes
a day talking to her children.

Are parents today more self-centered
than they were in the past?

What are the implications of these numbers:
0, 13, 26, and 39? The infant is 0 years, the
mother is 13, the grandmother is 26,
and the great grandmother is 39.

What do the following numbers mean:
28, 30, 2, and 4? Don't get married until
you're 28, wait at least 2 years before you
have children, only have 2 children,
and spread them 4 years apart.

Boys will be boys (if you let them).

No job is more important than parenting.

Are you teaching your son to get a good education in order to land a good job or to develop a good business?

Sons do not need parents to be their buddies and to party together. They need parents to act like adults, demand respect, and have a plan for their lives.

Does your son know that "sagging" pants reflect prison culture, where inmates can't wear belts? Does he also know that showing your underwear in prison notifies inmates that you've been raped and are available to other men?

What slavery did not do to the Black family has been done by crack cocaine.

It is easier to raise boys than to fix men.

When a boy is born, he needs female nurturing.

When he becomes older, he needs male mentoring.

The most important lesson to teach your son is self-discipline.

In studying great people, I found that someone in their family was crazy about them.

Teach your son to honor women.

Chapter 2: Trends

Moments in America for Black Children

- **Every 4 seconds** a public school student is suspended.*
- **Every 39 seconds** a public school student is corporally punished.*
- **Every 40 Seconds** a high school student drop out.*
- **Every minute** a child is arrested.
- **Every minute** a baby is born to an unmarried mother.
- **Every 2 minutes** a baby is born into poverty.
- **Every 4 minutes** a baby is born to a mother who is not a high school graduate.
- **Every 5 minutes** a baby is born without health insurance.
- **Every 5 minutes** a baby is born to a teen mother.
- **Every 7 minutes** a baby is born at low birthweight.
- **Every 13 minutes** a child is arrested for drug abuse.
- **Every 15 minutes** a child is arrested for violent crimes.
- **Every hour** a baby dies before his first birthday.
- **Every 5 hours** a child or teen dies in an accident.
- **Every 8 hours** a child or teen is killed by a firearm.

One Day in America Among Black Children

- 3 children or teens are killed by firearms.
- 22 babies die before their first birthdays.
- 64 second or subsequent babies are born to teen mothers.
- 96 children are arrested for violent crimes.
- 113 children are arrested for drug abuse.
- 217 babies are born at low birthweight.
- 289 babies are born to teen mothers.
- 276 babies are born without health insurance.
- 394 babies are born to mothers who are not high school graduates.
- 633 high school students drop out.*
- 643 public school students are corporally punished.*
- 697 babies are born into poverty.

- 1,158 babies are born to unmarried mothers.
- 1,286 children are arrested.
- 6,222 public school students are suspended.*

* Based on calculations per school day (180 days of seven hours each)

© 2007 Children's Defense Fund

- Five thousand preschool children are expelled annually; 90 percent are male.

- African American boys comprise 8.5 percent of the U.S. population but 33 percent of the students suspended, expelled, and placed in special education.

- Female students earn 60 percent of all As in American education. Male students earn 70 percent of all Ds and Fs.

- Ninety-nine percent of all preschool teachers are female. Ninety percent of all elementary school teachers are female. Sixty-four percent of all high school teachers are female.

- There are more than 800,000 African American males in college. There are more than 1.6 million African American females in college. African American females graduate at a 10 percent higher rate than African American males.

- Eight-six percent of NBA players are African American. Only 2 percent of engineers and doctors are African American.

- Twenty-five percent of Black male youth are unemployed.

- In 1980, one of every ten African American males was involved in the penal system. In 2007, one of every three African American males is involved in the penal system. It is projected that in 2020, two of every three African American males will be involved in the penal system.

- One out of every ten African American males is a victim of homicide.

- African American males comprise 12 percent of the U.S. population but represent 43 percent of all AIDS victims.[1]

High-School Graduation Rates

State	Black Male	White Male	Gap
Wisconsin	38%	84%	46%
New York	38%	76%	38%
Illinois	44%	84%	40%
Indiana	38%	71%	33%
Michigan	39%	73%	34%
Florida	31%	54%	23%
Nevada	32%	53%	21%
Nebraska	49%	85%	36%
Ohio	45%	75%	30%
Pennsylvania	50%	84%	34%
USA	45%	70%	25%
Oregon	47%	72%	25%
Delaware	44%	67%	23%
Minnesota	54%	85%	31%
Georgia	39%	54%	15%
Iowa	54%	83%	29%
South Carolina	40%	56%	16%
Alabama	45%	63%	18%
Colorado	52%	76%	24%
North Carolina	47%	65%	18%

Raising Black Boys

State	Black Male	White Male	Gap
Kansas	55%	79%	24%
Maryland	54%	78%	24%
Virginia	53%	73%	20%
Louisiana	51%	68%	17%
Texas	52%	71%	19%
Missouri	56%	78%	22%
California	55%	75%	20%
Mississippi	47%	60%	13%
Connecticut	59%	82%	23%
Kentucky	53%	69%	16%
Oklahoma	56%	74%	18%
New Mexico	53%	64%	11%
Massachusetts	61%	79%	18%
Alaska	54%	61%	7%
New Jersey	70%	92%	22%
Arkansas	62%	74%	12%
West Virginia	61%	71%	10%
Utah	73%	85%	12%
Rhode Island	66%	71%	5%
Arizona	85%	93%	7%

I speak at many graduations, and I've observed the following averages:

Grade	Male Graduates	Female Graduates
Kindergarten	12	12
8th Grade	47	53
High School	200	300
College	300	700

Please note that with each passing graduation, African American females are expanding the gap. We must save our boys.

Chapter 3: Parenting Quiz

Honestly grade yourself between an A and an F on the following questions. Show your paper to your son.

1. Have you helped your son develop career goals?

2. Are you consistent in your support of him?

3. Do you give your son quality time?

4. Do you give your son praise and encouragement?

5. Do you have high expectations of your son?

6. Do you monitor and check your son's homework?

7. How frequently do you visit your son's school?

8. Do you monitor your son's friends?

9. Do you monitor your son's music?

10. Do you monitor your son's television view-
    ing?

11. Is your son disciplined?

12. Do you give him affection?

13. Have you taught him his history and cul-
    ture?

14. How well do you listen to your son?

15. Have you provided him with good nutri-
    tion?

16. Does he receive adequate sleep?

17. How well does he do chores?

18. Do you take him on field trips?

19. Have you provided him a safe environ-ment?

20. Have you taught him morality and values?

Chapter 4: Black Families

It was another busy morning in the Davidson home. Grandmother Yvonne was preparing breakfast for Darryl, her grandson. Her daughter Marie had gone to work already. After work, Marie would go straight to class at the local college. On the days when she had class, she usually didn't get home until after 9:00 pm.

Darryl hurried to finish showering and put on his clothes. He was starving, and the smells coming up from the kitchen made his stomach growl. He ran down the stairs. "Morning, Grandmama!" he said. He looked for his homework to see who had initialed his paper, his mother or his grandmother.

Darryl asked, "When will I see Mama? Does she have class tonight?"

"You know this is your mama's late night," said his grandmother. "But don't worry, I'll be home when you get here. I'll have a nice dinner waiting for you, and I'll try my best to check your math problems. I never was any good in math, especially fractions and decimals, but I'll do the best I can."

Darryl smiled at his grandmother. He gobbled down his breakfast and flew out the door to get to school on time.

***

The school bus drove up the circular drive to the mansion. Richard got off the bus, pulled out his key, and opened the door to his beautiful house. As usual, no one was home. His mother was a senior purchasing agent for a Fortune 500 company. His father was a high-powered attorney and a partner in a law firm. They both worked long hours. He probably wouldn't see them until 7:00 or 8:00 pm this evening.

Richard went into the kitchen and made a sandwich. He took his snack to his beautiful bedroom and turned on the television to watch "106 & Park" and "College Hill" on BET. He opened his book bag and pulled out his books and notebooks. He had a lot of homework to do tonight. Richard is a master at doing homework while watching television.

***

Raising Black Boys

James was awakened early one morning by the angry sounds of his mother and her boyfriend arguing, again, downstairs. This was the third boyfriend in two years, and it bothered James. When James was only seven, one of her boyfriends had tried to beat him up. The man had been loud and disrespectful toward his mother. He had even pushed her around some, and James didn't like it. James paid for trying to defend his mother, and here she was, at it again.

More than anything, James wanted this new boyfriend to leave, just so he could go into the kitchen and make a quick breakfast before going to school. James wished he could live with his father, but unfortunately, his father didn't seem to want to spend time with him.

***

Thirteen-year-old Kevin lived in a foster home. He had lived in four foster homes over the past eight years. But today was his day. A family was interested in adopting Kevin. They wanted one final visit just to see if Kevin would adjust to them. The social worker told him that if he wanted a family, he'd better be on his best behavior during the interview. Once, years ago, another family had considered adopting Kevin. Unfortunately, they decided to adopt a girl. The father said, in front of Kevin, that it was nothing personal but girls were easier to raise than boys. Kevin never forgot that statement. He could understand a woman saying that, but why would a man say it's easier to raise a girl than a boy?

***

As the above stories illustrate, the Black family is not monolithic. The media has developed the image of the Black family over the years as poor and downtrodden. Many criticized Bill Cosby's TV family, the Huxtables, as an unrealistic portrayal of the Black family simply because they were wealthy and both parents were highly educated professionals. Many viewers felt the show promoted an anomaly—namely, a wealthy African American family. That is why when a program is aired about poverty or welfare, the statistics and images are mostly about the 16 million poor Blacks and Latinos in America while failing to mention the 24 million poor Whites.

The Black family is not monolithic. Consider the following statistics:

- Ten percent of African American families earn more than $100,000 per year.
- Twenty-five percent of African American families earn between $50,000 and $99,000 per year.
- Forty-two percent of African American families earn between $20,000 and $49,000 per year.
- Thirty-three percent of African American families earn less than $20,000 per year.

The Black family is not monolithic. Our boys are being raised in a variety of family configurations, and that transcends income.

- Thirty-two percent of African American children live in homes with either a biological parent and a stepmother or stepfather.
- Sixty-eight percent of African American children live in a single-parent home.
- Ninety percent of single-parent homes are headed by mothers. Ten percent of single-parent homes are headed by fathers. (Some 400,000 African American males are single parents, yet the media are silent.)
- Eight percent of African American children are reared by grandparents.
- Two percent of African American children are reared in interracial homes.
- Some 320,000 African American children are reared by foster parents.[2]

Black family income levels range from very poor to very rich and all levels in between. Black families live in all types of geographic settings, from the inner city to the suburbs. More than one million African American children are being reared in rural environments.

My goal is to address all Black families in this book because our boys deserve a fair and equitable chance to succeed in life, no matter their family structure and income, no matter where they are being raised. We should not assume that Black boys in affluent suburbs have a greater chance of success than in the inner city, rural communities, and small towns. If the adults in their lives are committed to their growth and development, they can succeed anywhere.

I am often asked by middle-income school districts to "fix" their Black male students. They mistakenly assume that income is the great equalizer, but that's not true. In fact, African American parents and educators have discovered, to their dismay, that the achievement gap is actually wider in affluent suburbs than in the inner city. Let's not assume that degreed parents who earn more than $100,000 a year and live in an affluent suburb will rear their son more effectively than a low-income, poorly educated, single mother in the inner city.

Throughout this book, we will look at the many risk factors affecting our boys across the board, and we will look at several powerful remedies to improve their academic performance and overall well-being. The remedies are surprisingly simple, as you'll see in the case of Sonya Carson, mother of Dr. Ben Carson, the best pediatric neurosurgeon in the country, if not the world. But it requires determination, commitment, and consistency from parents and schools.

The Black family is in a constant state of change. For better or worse, African American children are being reared in households headed by grandparents, foster parents, boyfriends and girlfriends, and fiancés.

Is marriage for White people only? Unfortunately, for some African American couples, shacking has become the norm. Boyfriends and girlfriends stay together for several years, and then they become fiancés for another several years. Marriage may or may not take place. Believe me, our boys are observing their parents' behavior, and they are taking mental notes.

Another factor that negatively affects our boys is the decreasing amount of time parents spend with them. Some tell me they do not see their parents all week. It's hard to fathom that our boys are not even talking to their parents. It has taken me a while to process this. When I was growing up, I received tremendous love and support from my mother and father, and that included daily conversations. Parents will say they love their children, but for a child growing up in a cold-hearted world, the definition of parental love *is* daily communication and attention.

Almost 70 percent of our children are being reared in single-parent homes. Not all single parents work from 7:00 am to 3:00 pm, 8:00 am to 4:00 pm, or 9:00 am to 5:00 pm. So what is a single-parent to do when the only job he or she can find requires working from 3:00 pm to 11:00 pm, 4:00 pm to 12:00 pm, or 11:00 pm to 7:00 am?

Schools hire me to speak to teachers and parents. They tell me the boys are broken, and they want me to provide the 10-step program that will "fix" the bad boys. I disagree with this premise. Our boys are not broken, but they do reflect the community and greater society. Bottom line: our boys, regardless of income, parent education, and residence, need adults in their lives who will make them their priority.

In the next chapter we will look at Black mothers. The future of the Black race lies in the hands of single-parent mothers.

Chapter 5: Mothers

The future of the Black race lies in the hands of single mothers, grandmothers, stepmothers, girlfriends, fiancées, foster mothers, and White mothers who had a child with a Black man. This chapter is for all females who are giving direction to Black boys. We begin with women because 68 percent of African American children are being raised in single-parent homes, most of which are headed by women. If we don't do anything else in this book, we must help mothers do a better job of raising their sons.

Black boys live in a variety of family structures. The media focuses on boys that are being reared by single mothers, but another common scenario is when the mother and father are divorced and they are now living with their new boyfriend/girlfriend. The boy has at least four adults in his life—a mother, father, girlfriend/fiancée/stepmother, and boyfriend/fiancé/stepfather.

What are the implications for Black boys living in these types of home environments? In some families, there may be poor communication and hostility among all adults involved. If the adults do not present a united front, child rearing becomes fragmented and inconsistent.

I want to commend all women who are involved in the development of their sons for doing a great job. It was not God's plan for you to be the provider, priest, and protector. Yet this is the very position you find yourselves in.

Parenting is a 24/7 job that lasts a minimum of 18 years, and your son is always watching you. Raising a son is challenging for single mothers because you were never a boy. You can never know what it means to be a man. Still, you are doing the best you can in often trying circumstances.

I would like to lift up two single mothers who both did an excellent job of raising their sons.

First, you must read *Gifted Hands: The Ben Carson Story,* pediatric neurosurgeon Ben Carson's wonderful autobiography. My favorite is the story he tells about being a failing fourth grade student in Detroit. Not only was he failing academically, he was failing psychologically. He had an awful temper. Yet Sonya Carson knew her son had potential. She knew he could be brilliant.

Sonya was a domestic, but her job did not limit her vision for her son. Can you imagine that? A domestic raises her son to be the best pediatric neurosurgeon in the country! Some parents in affluent suburbs are having a difficult time just keeping their sons out of jail.

Sonya noticed that the homes of her employers had many books and well-stocked libraries. It occurred to her that successful people are readers. After all, leaders are readers. Sonya took this to heart. To turn her son around, she decided that she would first turn off the television.

Note that Sonya did not *ask* Ben to turn off the television. She *told* him to turn it off. I'm concerned about parents who allow their sons to have televisions and cable in their rooms with a remote control and the option to watch at will.

Sonya told her son, "We are going to the library once a week. You will pick out two books, and you will read them." Note that Sonya did not ask Ben if he wanted to go to the library, nor did she ask him if he wanted to read the books. She clearly understood that she was the parent. She was not Ben's girlfriend. She was not going to nag him. She was on a mission.

Sonya also knew that boys will tell you they have done something when they haven't. To circumvent this, she made Ben write a paper about what he read. This was going to be a challenge because Sonya never went to school beyond the third grade. How was she going to read his report? She realized that she could not raise her son herself. Humbly, she asked her sister, Ben's aunt, to read the reports.

Sonya Carson did not have a PhD, a $100,000 salary, or a suburban home; still, she produced the best pediatric neurosurgeon in the country. She simply turned off the television, took him to the library, and made him read books and write reports. If Sonya Carson could do it, every mother, grandmother, stepmother, foster mother, White mother, girlfriend, and fiancée can do the same.

If you read the book or saw the movie, *The Mary Thomas Story,* then you know a little about Mary Thomas, the brilliant mother of Isaiah Thomas. Mary Thomas and her family lived in a rough inner city neighborhood in Chicago that was drug and gang infested.

Mary knew that her son's future was dependent on his peer group, so instead of letting Isaiah hang out on the corner with his friends, Mary invited them to hang out at her home. Amazingly, she also invited gang members. She did everything she could to provide alternatives to their gang lifestyles. With Isaiah's friends and the gang members at her house, it was difficult for him to get in trouble. Mary Thomas understood how important it is for mothers to monitor the peer group.

Unfortunately, there was an incident. The gang members did not respect Mary, and they were serious about recruiting Isaiah into their gang. They underestimated Mary Thomas' determination. She pulled out a shotgun and told them that the only gang in her house was the Thomas gang.

They looked at her. They looked at the shotgun. They saw how serious Mary Thomas was about protecting her son. They lost that showdown and walked away. Why is it that Mary was able to protect her son from gang members and the negative impact of the peer group when mothers who come into my office for counseling cannot? They say, "I can't do anything with him. He does not respect me."

Mother, you do not lose control overnight. That happens over a period of time.

There is a difference between being a single parent and single parenting. Many women have internalized the image of the poor single mother who has to raise her son by herself. As a result, they do not believe they can raise their sons to be men.

Being a single parent is a position; single parenting is a process. You are a single parent, but that does not mean you have to raise your son by yourself. In fact, there are many people and resources available that are ready, willing, and able to help:

- The child's father
- Your father
- Your grandfather
- Your brother
- Your uncle
- Your adult male cousins and nephews
- Your pastor, deacon, minister, usher, male church members
- Male co-workers
- Boy scouts
- Male rites of passage leaders
- 100 Black Men
- Mentoring programs
- Organized sports
- Male educators

Your son must have a male mentor! You are mistaken if you believe you can raise you son without a male mentor. Our community is experiencing problems with African American males, more so than with African American females, because the girls have their mothers in the home, and they have many female teachers. In contrast, almost 70 percent of our boys do not have their fathers in the home. Only 1 percent of America's elementary school teachers are African American males. It is possible for a Black boy to go from kindergarten to eighth grade without a male teacher. Can you imagine, a Black boy has not experienced a man in the home or the classroom, yet we naively expect him to become a man!

Mothers sometimes resist this idea. I don't know if the resistance stems from ignorance, arrogance, naiveté, ego, or simply male hatred. Whatever it is, it needs to be resolved. Your son's life is at stake. It is not a sign of weakness for a woman to make her son spend time with a male mentor.

Your son is not your property, and he should not be denied access to his father. The anger and disdain you may have gives you no right to deny him access to his father.

Do you really love your son? How can you say you love your son while denying him access to the most important man in his life?

If you have a problem with your ex, that's between the two of you. Do not run your negative agenda through your son. Mothers need to avoid the statement, "You're going to be just like your daddy" (in a negative context).

Mothers, if you think I'm hard on you, wait until the next chapter where I'll be much harder on fathers.

I know what you've gone through. The father may not have been there when you delivered the baby. Maybe he wasn't there for any of the early birthdays. He never called, never sent any money, but now all of a sudden, when the boy is an adolescent, he wants to begin to spend time with his son. Note that I didn't say *your* son. That could be the problem. You're having a problem acknowledging that the boy is not just your son. He's also his father's son.

Some mothers believe that fathers have to pay to play. I don't believe a mother has the right to tell the father, "If you can't pay, you can't see him." Money should not determine whether or not a father gets to spend time with his son.

I didn't say that raising a boy does not require money. But every boy needs a mentor, and the most important mentor in his life is his father.

The only reasonable exception is if the father is violent or emotionally unstable, and you think he would physically or emotionally harm your child. Even then I would recommend that the father find help and be allowed supervised visitations with social workers and psychologists present.

Most boys are not going to accept you denying them access to their father. In fact, they will hold you personally responsible. Children often defend the absent parent. Can you imagine, you have done everything for your son, but they still defend the one who is never around! Your son needs to see his father's shortcomings. Children are not stupid, but they need proper information. Later in life they can decide if they want to spend time with their father, and that decision will be based on their own observations, not yours.

The Two Critical Ages

Mothers, grandmothers, stepmothers, foster mothers, girl-friends, and fiancées—there are two critical ages in your son's life: ages 2 and 12.

Take a deep breath and get ready because your son is going to try you. The first time will take place during age 2. God gave all of His children free will, and some children have stronger wills than others. Some 2-year-old boys have stronger wills than their mothers.

I never will forget the time we were eating dinner one evening and our youngest son, who was a little older than 2, thought he would challenge us. We're very health conscious, which means green food is in abundance. That night we were having Brussels sprouts. He told us that he was not eating the Brussels sprouts, yet he had the nerve to ask for dessert. If we had let him have his way at age 2, who knows what we would have experienced at age 12.

My son lost the fight that night. We told him he was not going to receive ice cream, and he willfully replied, "Well, I'm not eating the Brussels sprouts." We then told him that he needed to go to bed.

The next morning, guess what he had for breakfast.

At the age of 2 he looked at us, we looked at him, and he smiled. He had issued his challenge and lost and was man (or boy) enough to smile about it and eat the Brussels sprouts.

Mothers, your sons are going to try you. It could be as early as 2 years of age, and you'd better be ready. A mother who says "I don't know what to do with my son" is a mother who has lost control of her child. This loss of control probably began when the boy was as young as 2 years old.

The second critical age is 12, the beginning of adolescence. Without a doubt, your son will try you again. If he wins this battle, you will lose the war. You will never be his parent again. You will be his girlfriend or buddy, but you will never be his parent. He will never respect you. I call it the showdown, a power struggle between sons and their parents, in this case the mother.

The good news is that the winner will not be determined based on size or gender. The rumor is that in order to be an effective parent of sons, you have to be male, tall, and young. I know a 4' 9" mother in her 60s who has a 6' 6" son in his 20s, and she can still tell him, "I brought you in here, and I will take you out." Being an effective mother of sons has nothing to do with his size or gender. In fact, as we'll discuss in the next chapter, there are incompetent, weak, Ahab (a weak husband in the Bible dominated by Jezabel) fathers who are less effective than strong-willed mothers with the skills and self-respect to get the job done.

Boys know by your eye contact and the tone of your voice when you mean business. Some mothers nag their sons. They ask them eight times to empty the garbage. Boys say, "She doesn't mean business. I can tell by the tone of her voice." And then there's the mother who will put down the telephone, pick up a skillet, and say to the boy, "One last time, empty the garbage." He does it because he knows she means business. She's still 4' 9" and female. What's the difference? The tone of her voice (and the skillet in her hand).

One day I was in church in Nacogdoches, Texas, with my grandmother. I was sitting in the balcony, and she was on the first floor. She could see I wasn't focused on the sermon and that I was talking. Her eyes literally pierced through 50 pews. Her eyes told me to come downstairs and sit with her.

Mothers, it has nothing to do with size or gender. It has everything to do with self-respect, eye contact, and the tone in your voice.

A boy will ask 999 times for something, and you must say no 999 times. It's like a boxing match. If he can wear you down for nine rounds, he can win it in the tenth. When the boy asks for the 1,000th time, he knows he's going to get what he wants.

Boys also know *when* to ask for something: when you're tired and when you're on the telephone. Remember, 8 percent of our children are being reared by their grandmothers. The boy is 13 and the grandmother is 70. She's tired. She's raised her children, and now she's doing it again. The boys know that.

Don't answer 999 times. Only answer 1 time. Once you give the answer, like a judge, that's it. Ignore them after that. When he knows you will consistently answer only once with no further discussion, you have earned his respect.

Among the many mothers I've counseled, the common denominator I've seen is that the mother is tired. Her son has worn her down, and it didn't have to be.

Many boys look at their mothers like a business deal. Let's negotiate. There's yes, no, and room in the middle to negotiate. Tell your son, "I want you back in the house at 10:00 pm." Like a good negotiator, he says, "What about 12:00?" His desire was 11:00 pm, but he said 12:00 because he wanted to negotiate. He thinks, well she says 10 and I say 12, why don't we agree to 11:00 pm. If he finds out he can negotiate with you, then you are no longer his mother. You are now his business partner.

You must clearly give your son one answer. Do not negotiate.

Many boys say they don't have a problem doing chores or whatever is asked of them. They want to know what is so magical about having to do it *now*. If the boy is watching a game or doing something he enjoys, consider his point. We all have our own rhythm. Some of us like doing chores early in the morning, some like doing them midday or in the evening. There's no harm in working out an arrangement with your son. Tell him what you expect. The bottom line is that he gets it done. As long as he gets it done, you don't have to be on his case. But if you find out that the floor was never mopped, the carpet was never vacuumed, the dishes were never washed, the homework was never done, then even the privilege of giving him the flexibility of when, not if he will do it, will be taken away from him.

Mothers, grandmothers, foster mothers, stepmothers, girlfriends, and fiancées, let me ask you one of the most important questions I will raise in this book: **how long can your son stay in your house?** Your answer will tell me how serious you are as a mother. I am concerned about a male staying in his mama's house in his 20s, 30s, 40s, 50s, and beyond. Some will never leave.

Let me ask you another question: do you realize that your little boy will be someone's husband and father some day? What you see in your son is what you will produce from your son.

If you see a future husband, that's what you will produce. If you see a future father, that's what you will produce. I am always amazed at women who are experts on the deficiencies in adult men while producing the same kind of flawed male in their sons!

For three decades I have asked the question, Do some mothers raise their daughters and love their sons?

Do they make their daughters come in early but not their sons?

Do they make their daughters study but not their sons?

Do they make their daughters do chores but not their sons?

Do they make their daughters go to church but not their sons?

Historically, the reason for this dynamic was slavery. Black males were castrated or lynched. We live in a world controlled by White men who believe in White male supremacy. The greatest threat to White men does not come from women, Black or White. The greatest threat to White men comes from Black men. The best way to destroy a Black male is at birth or during boyhood. Prison has become the new plantation.

Mothers overprotected their sons. They hid them in closets and under beds. They did whatever they could to protect their boys.

Is it true that females are more organized, responsible, and focused than Black men? Can we blame that on the White man? Did the White man make you have double standards for your son and your daughter?

Why would you tell a 9-year-old boy that he is the man of the house? Maybe you wanted to make him feel important. Because his father didn't stay, you bestowed upon him the title, "Man of the House."

Mothers, do you know what you just did? If he's the man of the house, then who are you?

If he's the man of the house, how can you tell him what to do?

If he's the man of the house, be careful about bringing your boyfriend over to spend the night because the man of the house does not like his mama bringing another man into *his* space.

If he's the man of the house, you can no longer discipline him.

If he's the man of the house, you will have to negotiate everything.

Later we will discuss in more detail the fact that too many mothers let the "man" of the house decide whether he wants to play basketball or participate in programs such as mentoring and rites of passage that will help his growth and development. Mothers are letting their sons make grown-up decisions before they have the wisdom and maturity to do so.

Incompetent mothers relinquish their parental authority when they tell their sons they are the man of the house. How can a 9-year-old boy be a man? How can a boy be a man if he's never spent time with one? Can you be something you have not experienced?

Who taught your son what it means to be a man? What is the job description of manhood? How can he wear a title he has not earned?

Mothers who raise their daughters and love their sons are raising their boys to be impotent. There's a reason why a male may never marry. He shacks with his girlfriend, and when she finally puts him out, he can always go back home to mother.

How long can your son stay in your house?

Let me take this further. Are you raising a pimp? A pimp is a male who takes advantage of women. He expects women to take care of him. He resents any woman holding him responsible for anything. I can share horror stories of mothers who work one, two, three jobs. She makes the money, pays the rent, and buys the groceries. When she tells her young son to help bring in the groceries from the car, the boy, the male, the pimp-in-training becomes irritated, even though this is food he will be eating.

Mothers who raise their daughters and love their sons over-protect their sons, and the sons know it. Everyone seems to know your son but you. Your son is convinced that the teacher, principal, counselor, social worker, coach, police, and other adults are all out to get him. You are always the one who comes to his rescue. Unfortunately, this is destroying your son.

I once saw a court trial where the mother slipped and said, "Well, he didn't mean to kill him." Even in court, she was still overprotecting her son.

Mothers, grandmothers, stepmothers, foster mothers, girl-friends, and fiancées must begin to give their sons some tough love. Don't let him go to bed until he has done his homework. Turn off the television. Make him do his chores. Believe it or not, doing chores early and well will determine whether your son will be able to secure and keep a job.

There are many reasons why so many Black males are un-employed. Twenty-five percent of Black male youths are un-employed. In some cities such as New York almost 50 percent of adult Black males are unemployed. While the global economy, racism, illiteracy, and poor education are factors, a major reason is irresponsibility.

How responsible is your son? Did you make him do his chores? Did you make him do them well? There is a relation-ship between how well your son mops, vacuums, and cleans up his room and how well he works on a job.

Many brothers can't keep a job because they can't get to the job on time. All an employer asks is that if your starting time is 9:00 am, you be there at 9:00 am.

I appeal to you, mothers, grandmothers, stepmothers, foster mothers, girlfriends, and fiancées, get your son up early to do chores on a regular basis. He needs to do chores, and he needs to do them well. This will develop within him a strong work ethic. As an adult, if he can't find a job, he will create his own. This is the type of man you want to develop.

My wife was serious about raising our sons well. Before they could go out to play, she inspected their rooms as though they were in the military. I wanted them to be able to go outside and play, but she insisted that no playing would take place until their chores were done and done well.

Finally, I want to ask, are you raising a sissy? I'm concerned about the increase in homosexuality. Some mothers understandably want to protect their sons from the street, but it is not healthy for boys to stay inside because you are afraid of the street.

Boys are aware of the pecking order in the street. The male peer group determines the hierarchy. Unfortunately, this pecking order is not based on report cards and test scores. It is based on how well you fight, play basketball, and handle yourself physically. It's all about demanding respect.

In no way am I suggesting that you allow your son to hang out from 3:00 pm to 10:00 pm. I would never encourage fighting or playing basketball until it's so dark you can't even see if the ball goes into the net. My point speaks to mothers who were never boys, never men. You cannot understand the intensity of the male pecking order because you never experienced it.

It is unacceptable that 86 percent of the NBA is African American but only 2 percent of the engineers and doctors. Something is wrong with this imbalance. We need more mothers like Sonya Carson that can produce a Dr. Ben Carson. But Ben Carson will also tell you he had to defend himself. I don't care what mothers do to protect their sons, at some point boys will have to defend themselves.

Mothers, if you really want to protect your sons, send them to a martial arts class. Not only will it teach them the art of self-defense but it will help them manage their anger.

They will learn the three aspects of manhood: spiritual, mental, and physical. There are three corners of a pyramid and three corners of manhood. Boys who are reared by the street are strong physically but are weak mentally and spiritually. Many mothers are raising their boys to be strong mentally, but they are weak physically. This book seeks to help our boys achieve a balance of the spiritual, mental, and physical.

Talk to Your Son

Words are awesomely powerful. God created the world with His Word.

God made us in His image; thus our words also have power. Your words can create or destroy your son. It is not an over-statement to say that the quality of your conversation will determine your success as a parent of a male child.

What do you and your son talk about?

Does he know what you expect of him?

How well do you listen to your son?

Honestly explore the quality of your conversation with your son. Remember, true conversation involves both talking and listening.

Parents, communication is crucial. We know that females share over 25,000 words daily. Unfortunately, your son may only share 10,000, and you don't want them all shared with his friends. Many parents talk at their sons and don't listen. Many boys feel tense when the conversation is formal. To relax your son, I suggest just sitting on his bed with no agenda and let him talk. If you must talk, start with topics he likes. I also recommend talking while playing games or shooting basketballs.

Fathers, now it is your turn. In the next chapter, we will explore what fathers must do to be the best role models they can be for their sons.

Chapter 6: Fathers

In 1913, One Ad Changed
The Face Of America's Middle Class.

'GOLD RUSH'
IS STARTED
BY FORD'S
$5 OFFER

Henry Ford recognized the value of a skilled workforce – regardless of race. And when Ford Motor Company became the first major corporation to pay African American workers equal pay for equal work, it helped give birth to the Black middle class.

I want to dedicate this chapter to the 32 percent of African American fathers who stay with their children. There are nearly 400,000 African American single-parent fathers. I want to see the television news open not with another murder or drug deal but with a young Black father going over his son's homework in preparation for the next day of school.

I am also dedicating this chapter to the fathers who stayed with both their children and wives and together are raising the children. These are the unsung heroes of our community.

Often when I speak, I'm inspired to ask all the fathers who are raising their children to stand up. I do this to acknowledge good men, and I want women to see that there are good men in our community.

This is a fact we men often forget! When talking to pastors, one of us will usually bring up the same negative statistics about Black men we hear in the media. We love talking about the number of brothers who are in prison and gangs, who are homeless or on drugs.

But the gospel represents Good News, which is that many brothers have not succumbed to the street, and they are in church. Black men need to hear some good news, especially when they come to church. They need inspiration to be even better men, husbands, and fathers.

It's one thing for the media to promote negativity in our community. It's another for us to perpetuate it.

This chapter is for fathers, grandfathers, stepfathers, foster fathers, boyfriends, fiancés, and all other men who are involved in raising our sons.

You are the greatest influence on your son's life. I cannot stress enough that your son is watching you 24/7.

Sometimes African Americans believe the greatest problem affecting them is racism and economics. I believe that *fatherlessness* is the second greatest problem facing us today. Later we'll discuss the greatest problem affecting our community, and that's the lack of spirituality. For now we'll look at fatherlessness, a plague in our community if ever there was one. If you look at all the woes in our society—drug addiction, teen pregnancy, illiteracy, grade retention, incarceration—the common thread running through them all is the absence of the father in a child's life.

Fathers

In my book *State of Emergency: We Must Save African American Males* I provide the following statistics that document the significance of fatherlessness:

- Sixty-three percent of youth that commit suicide are from fatherless homes.
- Ninety percent of all homeless and runaway children are from fatherless homes.
- Eighty-five percent of all children that exhibit behavioral disorders come from fatherless homes.
- Eighty percent of rapists motivated by displaced anger come from fatherless homes.
- Seventy-one percent of all high school drop outs come from fatherless homes.
- Seventy-five percent of all adolescent patients in chemical abuse centers come from fatherless homes.
- Seventy percent of juveniles in state-operated institutions come from fatherless homes.
- Eighty-five percent of all youths sitting in prisons grew up in fatherless homes.
- Eighty-two percent of teenage girls who get pregnant come from fatherless homes.

If we are going to successfully raise our boys, we need strong men to take parenting seriously.

There are many different types of fathers:

- Sperm Donors
- No-Show Dads
- Ice Cream Dads
- Dead Broke Dads
- Dork Dads
- Divorced Dads
- Stepfathers
- Daddies
- Single-Parent Dads

Unfortunately, our boys have more Sperm Donor, No-Show, Ice Cream, Dead Beat, Dork, and Divorced dads than Stepfathers, Daddies, and Single-Parent dads. Allow me to define my terms.

Sperm Donors. Unfortunately, in the Black community we have a large number of Sperm Donors, and they start young. Sperm Donors can become fathers as early as 12 to 13 years old.

Sperm Donors don't stay long. They only stay long enough to make the babies, approximately 18 seconds.

Sperm Donors define their masculinity based on the quantity of children they create, not the quality of their childrearing. If we had a strong village, we would deal with these Sperm Donors in no uncertain terms. We would visit them and ask about their intentions toward the female and the child. We would make them do right by mother and child.

There's nothing wrong with our sons. The problem is with Sperm Donors.

No-Show Dads. This father promises to pick the child up on Saturday at noon, but he never shows. We can't blame this behavior on the White man. How can a man promise to pick his son up and not show? He is a liar, and his word cannot be trusted.

The son wants to be with his father and wonders if he is to blame for the father's bad behavior. This father has a deep character flaw that may negatively impact the son's ability to trust and respect authority figures. Throughout his life, the son will experience the deep wound of low self-esteem because he feels unwanted by the most important man in his life.

Imagine how a mother feels. She is the one who must pick up the pieces after each disappointing no show. She loves her son. She sees how excited he is as he waits for his father to pick him up. Maybe he's been talking about his dad all week. She's worried he's going to be hurt, so she tells him things like, "Don't get your hopes up too high, honey. Sometimes things happen."

On the big day, he packs his bag. He watches the clock. He sits by the door. He asks his mother, "Has he come yet?

Did he call?" Mother sees the look on his face when it begins to sink in that father's not going to come. Again.

What's a mother to do? She's trying to be responsible in allowing her son to spend quality time with his father. Is she hurting her son or helping him by keeping the door open for a No-Show Dad?

This is just the kind of experience that can break a boy's spirit. Many of our boys' spirits have not been broken by school. They have been broken by Sperm Donors and No-Show Dads.

Ice Cream Dads. These fathers show up, but they feel guilty, so they buy their boys things. Things are a poor substitute for quality time, and they know it. These fathers take their sons to baseball, football, and basketball games, to amusement parks, restaurants, ice cream parlors, and department stores. What they have not learned is that nothing can replace the time a father spends with his son.

Dead Broke Dads. You may be a Dead Broke Dad, but that does not mean you have to be a Dead Beat Dad. You can have empty pockets but still be a responsible, strong, loving father for your son.

Mothers, I've said it before: the pay to play philosophy is wrong. Don't let issues with child support prevent your son from being with his father. Also, keep the discussions about money away from the children. Only discuss child support with your ex.

For this scenario to work, mother and father must work as a team. This can be difficult if child support is delinquent. Still, if you love your son, allow him to continue to see his father. Mothers, you may have to encourage the father to see his son. He may be tempted to stay away because he feels ashamed about his financial situation. Unfortunately, Dead Broke Dads believe the hype. They believe that you cannot be a man without money. I understand the logic here. If you live in a capitalistic, patriarchal country like the United States, it is difficult to be a man without income. Being able to financially provide for, protect, and spiritually guide those who depend on you is the essence of being a man. Mothers, it may really go against the grain, but for the sake of your son, please allow them to continue to spend time with each other.

Dead Broke Dads, do not allow this economic system to break your spirit. Do not allow your lack of income to separate you from the most important job in your life, which is to raise your son.

Dork Dads. Also known as Peter Pan Dads, these fathers have an Ahab spirit. Ahab was that evil king of Israel who married the infamous Jezebel. He allowed that woman to run him completely.

Dork Dads are physically in the home, but they are not emotionally present. They let their wives make all the decisions. After a while, children know who to go to when they want something, and it's not their father. At best, Dork Dads are the financial providers, but that's about it. After spending eight hours at work, their main job is to sit in their favorite chair and watch television. The supervision and nurturance of the children falls solely on the shoulders of the mother.

Boys are suffering because of Sperm Donors, No Shows, Ice Cream Dads, Dead Broke Dads, and Dork Dads. What they need are more of the following dads.

Divorced Dads. These dads have made a decision. They may be divorced from their wives, but they would never divorce their children. We need to understand the psyche of a man who is so resentful and full of vengeance that he would hurt his son. What kind of man would stay away from his own son? Knowing that the mother loves the son so much, is he trying to hurt her by hurting the child? What kind of man would do that?

We use three words to describe a male: male, boy, and man. A person is born male. It requires nothing of you to be born male. This is purely a function of genetics.

The next stage is boyhood. Males become boys, and boys like to play. When they're younger, boys play with balls, trucks, and cars. When they're older, they play with women and children. They can be 40 years old and still be a boy.

Divorced Dads are not boys. They have made a decision that regardless of what happened with the mother, it will never prevent them from spending time with their children. I could write an entire book about the challenges of being a Divorced

Dad. I have listened to and counseled numerous Divorced Dads who agonize over what's going on in their sons' lives. He's a Christian, she's not. He believes in academics, she doesn't. He believes in financial responsibility (savings, mutual funds, and stock options), she believes in spending everything she has. He believes in marriage, she believes in shacking. She believes in time out, he believes in the belt. He believes in structured activities, she believes in letting the son hang out. (The same anxieties apply to Divorced Mothers.)

The reality is that divorce is hard on everyone, especially children. Divorce has cost sons a lot of lost time with their fathers.

Stepfathers. With the divorce rate in the Black community at nearly 70 percent, many families have become blended. Stepparenting is also one of the major reasons for divorce the second time around. It is a real challenge to come into a child's life in the latter years. It is even more challenging when the biological parents are still present and some of their insecurities and issues have not been resolved.

I have a problem with a Sperm Donor who stays 18 seconds and receives the title of "father" while the stepfather, who stays 18 years or more, is called "step." You don't measure parenting based on biology. You base it on sociology and psychology.

Stepfathers, there are three factors that will affect your parenting of your stepson:

1. How old was the child when you came into his life?
2. How much time does the son spend with his biological father?
3. What decisions have you and your wife made regarding your parental rights and responsibilities?

It is a different experience for a stepfather if he comes into the family during the son's infancy versus when the son is 16 years old. It is a different experience if you are a custodial stepfather versus seeing the child every other weekend. Whether or not the biological father is present affects the experience as well.

Stepfathers, whatever the experience, whatever amount of time you have with the child, make the best of it. Your conversation could be just the thing that's needed to shape your son into the man he will become one day.

Daddies. I commend fathers who stay with their spouses and children. I wish more people were aware of what you are doing. You represent the best in our race, and your story needs to be told. I love watching a daddy with his wife and children. Boys learn how to treat their wives from these experiences. I adore watching a daddy listen to and nurture his wife and children. We need a media that will saturate us with daddies.

Your relationship with your son transcends income and education. We assume that only the low-life brothers, the unemployed brothers, the illiterate and uneducated brothers walk away from their children. That is not true. There are males with PhDs, earning six figures, who don't take care of their children. On the other hand, there are poorly educated brothers working at McDonald's who are excellent, nurturing fathers.

Single Fathers. Last but surely not least is the Single Father who assumed total responsibility for his children when the mother walked. Not only are you the provider, protector, and priest, you provide the mothering aspect of parenting, the nurturance and emotional stability all children need.

As the custodial parent, you are raising your son with or without the mother's assistance, and you have demonstrated that men too can develop a strong bond with their children. I take my hat off to you because you're doing a tremendous job. I just wish your story was told more often to inspire other brothers to realize the difference they can make in their children's lives.

There are three main aspects of fatherhood: provider, priest, and protector. Unfortunately, many men define their manhood purely based on economics. No money, no manhood.

The priest aspect of manhood is critical. I encourage you to read my two books *Adam, Where Are You? Why Most Black Men Don't Go to Church* and *Developing Strong Black Male Ministries.* Church attendance reflects the fact that men tend to underestimate the importance of the priestly role; 66 percent of females and only 34 percent of males attend church. Men, we must do better.

In your household, is prayer taking place? Is Bible study taking place? Are these activities being initiated and led by the mother or father? When a child becomes saved, only 4 percent of their family will give their lives to Christ. When a mother is saved, only 17 percent of her family will give their lives to Christ. **When a man is saved, more than 90 percent of his family will give their lives to Christ.**

Some women make compromises: she's saved, her husband's not. She goes to church, her husband doesn't. She makes her daughter go to church but not her son.

When a man is priest of his home, there are no compromises. When a man becomes saved, everybody goes to church—the wife, the daughter, the son, the dog, the cat, the roaches! There is something wonderful about a man who takes the priestly role seriously.

Fathers, God is going to hold you accountable on Judgment Day if you do not take this role seriously. It is your job to teach your children about the Lord. It is your job to teach your children the power of prayer and the Word and to be the example of a godly man.

The third aspect of being a father is that of protector. Inner city neighborhoods are crumbling because the fathers are missing in action. Some inner city neighborhoods are filled with women, elders, and children—but no men. Can you imagine a neighborhood where there are women, elders, and children but no men between 25 and 45 years old? When this takes place, boys form gangs and take charge of the neighborhood. Gangs are formed when fathers do not take their rightful position at home and in the neighborhood.

I used to live and work in Baltimore. I never will forget the neighborhood known as Little Italy, which is next to the ghetto. In the ghetto women, elders, and children know it is not safe to walk the streets at noon. In Little Italy, however, elderly women can walk the streets at midnight and not be harassed. In Little Italy the men take their role as protector seriously.

Raising Black Boys

Remember what Mary Thomas had to do to protect Isaiah. She should not have had to face those gangsters by herself. That was the job of Mr. Thomas, but he wasn't there. Our problem is that we live in neighborhoods where men have not taken seriously the responsibility of being the protector.

In *Boyz n the Hood* there is a powerful scene where the mother realizes she can no longer raise her son by herself. She hands over all custodial rights to the father. Later in the movie, the son is in a car with friends who are planning to kill someone. The son has a decision to make. Will he ride and die with his partners or will he get out of the car? He decides to get out of the car. What prompted him to make this wise decision, and why did the other boys go ahead with their foolish plan? The other boys were fatherless. The reason why he got out the car and went on to Morehouse College was because he had a daddy who took his role of provider, priest, and protector seriously. As a result, he saved his son's life.

Many fathers make a critical mistake. Because of their large male ego, they want to live their lives through their sons. Fathers must search their souls and make sure they are not living vicariously through their sons. They should never use their sons to achieve their own unfulfilled dreams.

I'm concerned when I see three generations of a single family assuming the same career such as pastors, police officers, soldiers, accountants, or any other walk of life. Not that this should never happen, but I wonder if the sons are being given the opportunity to develop themselves in an area they want to pursue.

Kahlil Gibran wrote in his book *The Prophet,* "Your children are not your children. They come from you, but they don't belong to you." We need to realize that our children, our sons, belong to God. They do not belong to us. Let your son decide on his own what he wants to be.

We see this also being played out in the names given to sons, the Jr.'s, the III's, IV's, and VI's. I don't see this with mothers, but I sure see this with fathers. What is it about the male ego? Your son is not yours. The sooner you understand that, the sooner you and your son can have a relationship that's balanced and healthy.

Finally, women complain all the time that men don't talk to them enough. Actually we talk, but only about things that matter to us. Sometimes we just don't want to talk. Still, we must be respectful of the needs of others.

In fact, don't let her complaint trickle down to your son. He needs quality conversation with you, too. He needs to know about your experiences, your world view. As priest, you must talk to him about God. Teach him how to pray.

Let your son hear you talk to others respectfully. He is watching you and listening to every word you say. If you can only manage 10,000 words with your son this week, make them count. Jesus said that we will be held responsible for every idle word (Matthew 12:36). He was speaking about the Day of Judgment, but there is also a more immediate accounting in the mind of your son. Your words can build him up or tear him down, so choose your words carefully.

Chapter 7: Denial

It is difficult to admit that you need
someone whom you have never (or seldom)
experienced.

He has never experienced a man in authority.

Their mother told them that they were the
man of the house.

If they are the man of the house,
they do not need, nor value, a male teacher,
counselor, dean, administrator, coach, mentor,
or any other male in authority.

He does not need a man to provide
because their mother is the provider.

They do not need a man to teach them how to
farm or work in a factory because
those jobs are obsolete.

He does not need a man to teach them how to develop skills in the area of information systems because either a woman can do that or they do not value those skills.

They do not need a man to teach them about sexuality because they "think" that *life* has adequately educated them.

He does not need a man to teach them how to rap, play basketball, or fight because their friends can teach them.

They do not need a man to teach them how to drive because schools provide drivers' education classes.

He does not need a man to teach them how to repair things because America has decided that it's cheaper just to discard the old and purchase the new (all from overseas).

They do not need a man to teach them
how to treat a lady because certain media,
as well as their peers, have convinced them
that the female doesn't desire nor deserve
to be treated with respect.

He does not need a man to teach them how to
be a father because they "unknowingly"
have decided to be a sperm donor.

Finally, because their mother appointed
them the *man of the house*,
they may never have a need to leave!

Chapter 8: Goals

What goals do you have for your son? What is your 5- 10- 15-year plan for your son?

For you?

What strategies or plans do you have in place to develop your son?

Proverbs 29:18 says, "Where there is no vision, the people perish." What vision do you have for your son?

Does your son know the goals you have planned for him?

Jeremiah 29:11 says, "I alone know the plans I have for you, plans of prosperity and not disaster, plans for a future that you have hoped for." I recommend that you place this scripture in your son's room on a poster. He should read this on a regular basis. God has a plan for your son's life.

In the Bible, Habakkuk 2:2 says, "Write the vision and make it plain." Many of us have goals, but they are not written down. If your son has not achieved any goals, they may not have been properly communicated.

Consider the great work that Earl Woods did with Tiger Woods, what Richard Williams did with Venus and Serena, what Earl Graves has done with his sons. While fathers should not live vicariously through their children, I do want to highlight the power of a parent with a vision, a goal. Woods, Williams, and Graves demonstrate that children will achieve the vision if it is clearly discussed.

If you don't know, or care, where you're going, any road will take you there. Our sons make mistakes because they have nothing to lose. You're not at risk because you come from a single-parent, low-income, or inner city home. You're at risk when you don't have any goals.

A principal at an inner city middle school had a powerful one-word mission statement for her students: college. Her students would never forget that mission statement because it was written down everywhere and verbally reinforced at assemblies.

Hang a picture of Morehouse College in your son's room. Have literature about Morehouse in your son's bedroom for him to read. During spring and summer breaks, take field trips to Morehouse and other colleges so that your son will see firsthand his future: college. I'm not a graduate of Morehouse, but I've spoken there many times and respect the school very much. It is our only Black male college, and they are doing a fantastic job. If your son catches the vision of college as early as infancy, he will surely go to college.

Graduations are a time for rejoicing, but I get concerned when, at kindergarten, eighth grade, and high school graduations, the parents have rented limousines and have planned expensive parties and dinners when really all your son needed was a hug, a hearty handshake, and a pat on the back. The student hasn't done anything significant yet! He was supposed to graduate from kindergarten, elementary school, and high school! Remember the mission: college. So the main event must be your son's college graduation.

Post the following phrase in your son's room: One Down, Two to Go. When he graduates from high school: Two Down, One to Go.

We need to raise the bar with our sons. Many parents brag that their sons are not in jail. They believe that avoiding jail is significant. I'm aware that one of every three African American males is involved in the penal system, but we shouldn't focus our vision and goals on prison avoidance. The bar needs to be higher than avoiding prison.

Many of our boys believe that their four best career options are the NBA, rap, the NFL, or being the first drug dealer never to be caught. Parents must raise the bar for their sons.

Have your son type his one-year, three-year, five-year, ten-year, and fifteen-year plans, and have him hang this important document in his room. Maybe the reason why our sons do not have goals and plans is because many adults do not have multiyear plans. The problem is not with our sons. It is with the adults.

Right now, write down your plans for the next one, three, five, ten, and fifteen years. Your son has every right to say, "I'm writing my plan. What's your plan? What are you going to be doing five and ten years from now?" Remember, the people without a vision will perish.

Also in your son's room should be a poster with the numbers 28, 30, 2, and 4. The numbers are not as important as the concept.

Here's the lesson for your son: do not get married until you're **28** years old, when, hopefully, you're feeling good about yourself. Wait at least **2** years (30) before you have children, and don't have children until you and your spouse have discussed it. Only bring into the world that number of children you can take care of , and spread them **4** years apart so that they can receive enough lap time and nurturing. The financial benefit is that, hopefully, you will not have more than one child in college at the same time.

This plan for having children is much better than the haphazard way Sperm Donors have children, often starting at 16 years of age and conceiving one or two every year thereafter. The sooner your son learns these numbers, the better.

Take the time to list the top four goals you'd like your son to achieve.

Would you like him to have a personal relationship with Jesus?
Would you like him to earn a college degree?
Would you like him to earn a large income?
Would you like him to be responsible?
Would you like him to be a husband and father?

It hurts me when I ask parents, "So, how's your son doing?"
They'll say, "He's in college."
"How many hours is he taking?"
"He's taking six."
Then I'll ask, "Well, is he working?"
"Oh, he's working. He's working about ten hours a week."
Here we have a parent, usually a mother, who feels her son is doing extremely well. He has avoided prison, he's in college, and he's working. We need to raise the bar. Avoiding prison, finishing six hours of courses, and ten hours of work does not represent success. Your son's potential is much higher than that.

Your son needs to be taught the distinction between being a male, a boy, and a man. Another poster (your son's room is going to be full of posters) should state:

Males – are born
Boys – play
Men – work

Parents need to help their sons understand the distinction between a boy and a man. In America, many of our boys do not know when they become a man. Later we will discuss rites of passage programs that deal with this issue. If adults do not define for boys what it means to be a man, then boys will mess it up every time.

Some boys think being a man is having sex, making babies, collecting numerous women, drinking, smoking, staying out late, and driving fast. In some communities, manhood is based on when you go to jail or when you kill someone.

Males without vision or goals think like that. We need adults to redefine for our boys what it is to be a man. Our boys need to be clear on the distinction between boyhood and manhood. You can be 40 years old and still be a boy. You can be 18 years old and be a man.

Successful Jewish and Asian communities uphold certain standards for their children. In Asian cultures, some of the values they instill in their children include:

- Love of learning
- Family pride
- Delayed gratification and sacrifice
- Respect for elders
- Academics over popularity.

How do you know if you're successfully raising your son? Simply assess the glow in his eyes, his innocence, curiosity, and love for learning. Has his spirit been broken?

Does your son have "it?" Oprah once said that the typical student in her school in South Africa has "it." When pressed to define "it," she pinpointed confidence, leadership, and the refusal to give up.

We need to help our sons develop this "it." We can monitor "it" by their spirit. Parents need to do everything they can to make sure no one ever breaks their sons' spir*it*. Note that "it" is within spir*it*. Moreover, we must make sure our sons never lose "it."

Chapter 9: The Power of Words

The quality of conversation in your home is an important indicator of how successful your son will be in life. Proverbs 18:21 says, "Death and life are in the power of the tongue."

Satan will tell you, "Sticks and stones will break your bones, but words will never hurt you." That's a lie. In the powerful series *The Law of Confession*, which I encourage you to purchase from Living Word Christian Center in Forest Park, Illinois, my Pastor, Bill Winston, teaches that words are more powerful than bombs.

Take the case of Malcolm Little. I didn't say Detroit Red or Malcolm X. I said Malcolm Little. He was a brilliant eighth-grade honor-roll student. One day in school, his teacher asked him what he wanted to be when he grew up. Malcolm said he wanted to be a lawyer. I believe Malcolm would have been one of our best. Unfortunately, his teacher told Malcolm he couldn't be a lawyer and cruelly advised him to be a carpenter. This brilliant eighth-grade honor-roll student was initially destroyed by the words of his teacher. Words turned an honor roll student into a drug dealer and criminal.

Some parents say to their children, "Mama never was any good in math" or "Daddy never was good in science." Maybe that explains why, when I ask young people if they're better in sports or science, they choose sports. When I ask if they're better in music or math, they choose music. When I ask if they're better in rap or reading, they choose rap.

Parents, if you have a deficiency in a subject, please keep it to yourself. You don't want your son to think his math or science deficiency is genetic. They'll begin to believe that Whites are better in math and science and Blacks are better in sports and music. In the chapters on peer pressure and Africentricity, we'll look at the phenomenon of our youth associating being smart with acting White. Since our youth don't want to "act White," they resist taking advanced placement and honors classes. Urgently, we must teach them that being smart is acting African. They need to know that Imhotep, not Hippocrates, was the first doctor.

Mothers, your words have power, so watch what you say to your son. Some mothers say, "You're going to be just like your daddy"—and it's not meant as a compliment. Other mothers go further and make derogatory statements about what the father has or has not done.

I've heard parents curse their children out and then naively think they can make up for it by making sweet potato pie, hoping all will be forgotten. How many elders today are still reflecting on what was said to them as children?

Researchers Hart and Risley wanted to find out if income level had anything to do with the kinds of words and statements children are exposed to. They discovered that the basic difference was in the number of discouragements—"prohibitions and words of disapproval compared with the number of encouragements and words of praise and approval. By age three, the average child of a professional heard about 500,000 encouragements and 80,000 discouragements. For the welfare children, the situation was reversed. They heard on average about 75,000 encouragements and 200,000 discouragements."[3]

One day our grandson was visiting, and he recited his alphabet well. He said, "Clap for Phoenix! Clap for Phoenix!" Of course, we did. It was so cute because we knew that this is what he had been taught in preschool. When you do something well, you're given words of encouragement.

I'm a tennis player, and I often see parents teaching and encouraging their young children how to play. The child may hit the ball over the fence or up in the sky, but the fact that he hit it at all is reason for encouragement.

Words are powerful.

Too many of our boys are stigmatized during the tender preschool years as "bad boys." Can you imagine, a two-, three-, or four-year-old being called a "bad boy"? You must protect your son's spirit. Parents may not be aware that their son is being called "bad boy" in the day care program they are paying for. We are often paying people to destroy the spirits of our children.

The Power of Words

In *The Law of Confession*, Pastor Winston teaches that you cannot rise above the level of your confession. This is why goal setting is so important. You cannot go any higher than your goal, vision, and confession. If we tell our boys the best they can do is get a high school diploma, stay out of jail, and earn $10 an hour, they will not rise any higher than that confession. You need to say what God says. If God says, "I can do all things through Christ who strengthens me" (Philippians 4:13), and if all means all, then you can excel in math and science. You can ace any test.

Mark 9:23 says, "If you can believe, all things are possible for those who believe." That explains why Barack Obama, presidential candidate and author of *The Audacity of Hope*, has the audacity to believe he can run for president. He was not the first African American to believe so. The lesson we can learn from Shirley Chisholm, Jesse Jackson, Al Sharpton, and Barack Obama is that it's important to raise the bar. Our children need to believe they can be a congressman, senator, mayor, governor, or president. Let's no longer limit our children by speaking destructive words around them.

I wish parents could hear some of the things teachers say about their children in the teachers' lounge. I believe the most important room in the school is not the classroom; it's the teachers' lounge. Teachers need to understand the power of their words. Just because the Bible was taken out of schools doesn't mean that spiritual principles are no longer in effect. In fact, teachers would be much more effective with our boys if they would motivate and inspire them with empowering words.

Parents, help your son develop a confession that projects where he would like to go in life. A confession is like prayer: you make it on a regular basis. It is a statement of your faith. The beauty of confession is that after awhile, you begin to believe what you're saying about yourself. When you believe, your entire life realigns with that belief. This is a law that will work for you, and it will work for your son. Goal setting and confession are two of the greatest gifts you can give to your son.

I was at a park one day and listened to a conversation between a Jewish mother and another woman. The woman said, "Oh, your sons are just so handsome!" The mother shrugged it off and said, "My 2-year-old, that's my doctor. My 3-year-old, that's my lawyer." The power of words. As early as 2 and 3 years of age, she's planting seeds in her sons.

Intrigued, the woman asked the 3-year-old about his career plans. He said, "I'm going to be a lawyer!" As adults, our job is to sow seeds. Hart and Risley's findings are disturbing because they reinforce so many stereotypes, especially in the areas of income and education. Low-income single-parents who do not have a college degree need to realize how important it is to encourage their children. We don't need to chastise and scold on such a regular basis. We need to "clap for Phoenix!"

There is another source of negative words that aims straight for the hearts of our boys, and that's gangsta rap. The message is in the music. There's a reason James Brown sang "I'm Black and I'm proud." Young people try to convince me they're not into the lyrics, just the beat. The truth is, when our children listen to this music, their souls absorb the lyrics like a sponge. If the message is in the music, then we're in trouble. Our children never should be exposed to the profane words of gangsta rap. We tell our sons not to curse, but we allow them to listen to music that is infused with derogatory words. No wonder they are confused.

What is your ratio of praise to criticism? From now on, increase the praise you give to your son and watch him light up like the sun. Also, never curse at your child or in front of him again. Remove the N, B, and H words from your vocabulary. The most important barometer to measure and evaluate your son is his spirit. If words are as powerful as bombs, you can no longer afford to destroy your son's spirit with your words.

Chapter 10: Household Items and Chores

By observing the contents of your home for five minutes, I can tell you the kind of child who will come out of your home. I've observed a few more things about our homes as well.

For example, doctors and engineers need certain items in their homes. Ballplayers and rappers need certain items in their homes. What you put in your house tells me something about your values.

I've been in homes where there's not one book in the house. Or the only book they have is a Bible, and that has been opened to Psalms 23 for decades. Your house should stimulate reading. You should have library books that your son chooses, magazines about rap, sports, cars, electronics, comic books, and whatever else he wants to read that you feel is morally acceptable.

There are more luxury cars parked in front of homes in the inner city than in the suburbs. Your car note should never exceed the rent or mortgage.

A parent will claim he doesn't have a dollar for a field trip while purchasing a $7 pack of cigarettes.

Do you have more CDs in your house than books?

Do you have more DVDs in your house than books?

Do you have more televisions than computers? A television is a toy, and a computer is a tool.

I've seen children destroy their toys in less than a week. If only parents had bought them, not necessarily a hammer or screwdriver, but some toy that has utilitarian value, like blocks or Legos. Something they can use to build things. With blocks they can build towers as well as read the numbers and letters. The purpose of a toy is pleasure. A tool provides pleasure and has an educational benefit as well.

Is your house designed to produce a scholar or a drop out?

Below are items every household should have. Read the list carefully and check off the items that are in your home.

- Children's books
- Adult books
- Black history books
- Library card(s)
- Academic games (Scrabble, checkers, chess, Uno, Monopoly, Black history games, etc.)
- Black history posters
- Dictionary
- Thesaurus
- Computer
- Software
- Internet access
- Musical instruments
- Telescope
- Chemistry set

The bedrooms of many boys are virtual bachelor pads. These rooms are stocked with a television (cable access), DVD player, CD player, Genesis, X Box, Play Stations 1 and 2, microwaves, and mini-refrigerators. As a result, the boys never have to come out and interact with other family members.

This may explain why some boys will never leave home. They have a private apartment in the house, and they are not paying rent!

Yet with all these toys and games, where are the books? Where's the chemistry set?

Computers with Internet access have become a necessity of life. Parents need to rigorously monitor how much time their son is spending on the computer for homework and how much time is being used to download music or pornographic pictures. If the computer is primarily being used to download music or pictures, then you should reconsider your son's use of the computer.

For many children, the discipline of "time out" is not all that disappointing, especially if it means spending a couple of hours or several days in a fully stocked bedroom.

Household Nutrition

Your son's diet will determine whether he will die of heart disease, cancer, or diabetes or whether he will live a long and healthy life. In my book *Satan, I'm Taking Back My Health* I document that one of every two Americans will die of heart disease. One of every three will die of cancer. One of every six will die of diabetes.

Doctors usually want to determine if heart disease, cancer, or diabetes run in your family. While, unfortunately, many in my family have died of those diseases, I have to remind the doctor that they have nothing to do with me because I eat out of a different pot.

If you live in a household where pork, bacon, and sausage are served for breakfast, baloney and salami are served for lunch, and ribs and ham are served for dinner, that may explain why high blood pressure, cancer, and diabetes run in your family. When you change the pot, you change the outcome.

Are you protecting your son from heart disease, cancer, and diabetes?

Look at all the food you have in your house. What percent of the food is meat? What percent is carbohydrates? What percent is fruit and vegetables? What percent of your fruit and vegetables is actually raw? What percent is in cans and boxes?

What percent of your son's diet is green? The magic green color in vegetables is not from money but chlorophyll.

Have your son take a multiple vitamin every day. I'm proud of the fact that I've never missed a day's work in my 34-year career, thanks to God, diet, and exercise.

Too many parents have relinquished the responsibility of being the adult as it relates to their children's diet. If you ask them which they would prefer, a doughnut or Brussels sprouts, cake or greens, I think you know what they will choose.

If only the gangsta rappers who are raising our sons would spread the word about the importance of eating healthy foods.

Fast food chains are a major source of disease and illness in our community. We cannot allow McDonald's, Wendy's, Burger King, and others to raise our sons. That is our responsibility.

Chores

There is an interesting relationship between chores and adult male employment. The words you say, the items you have in your house, the food you give your children, and whether you require them to do chores and how promptly and well they do them literally determine whether your son will be able to hold a job.

It's disappointing that so many African American males cannot secure and maintain a job. I have friends who are employers, and they are committed to hiring African Americans, but they struggle with hiring males because of their poor work ethic. You don't acquire a work ethic on your 21st birthday. This is one value that must be instilled early.

Ages	Chores
2–6 years	Make the bed, sweep, put toys away
7–11 years	All of the above, plus mop, wash dishes, vacuum
12–18 years	All of the above, plus wash clothes, cook a full course meal, babysitting

Boys do not leave their mamas' houses because they don't know how to run a household. Can you imagine, the boy (I didn't say man) is 40 years old and still does not know how to separate the white clothes from the colors and darks and what temperatures to use on different fabrics.

The only thing the boy knows how to make is a cheese sandwich.

Look at your son's bedroom. You can tell an awful lot about how effective you are as a parent by looking in your son's bedroom. It's true that many boys actually do their homework and then they can't find it. Weeks after the homework was due, they find it under the bed somewhere. There is a rumor that women are more organized than men. When do you think that starts?

Does your son make up his bed on a regular basis?

How well does your son clean his room? He doesn't believe that since you were once a child, you know all the best hiding places in the bedroom (under the bed and in the closet). So rather than giving the room a thorough cleaning, he hides all his junk either under the bed or in the closet. Some things never change.

We need to help our sons become better organized. There is a 10 percent differential between African American females and males graduating from college. An African American male may have the GPA and test scores to be admitted into college, but because he lacks discipline, responsibility, and organizational skills, he does not graduate. That did not start on his 18th birthday.

In some households, cleaning, cooking, doing laundry, making beds, and running errands are considered women's work. This could not be further from the truth. When your son moves out to live on his own, how will he take care of himself? I wonder how many males have rushed into relationships with girlfriends, fiancées, and wives because they had no household management skills or they got really hungry. They couldn't take care of themselves.

Mothers, do you see your sons as future husbands and fathers? Can you imagine your son—someone who is a slob—becoming a husband! He just throws things all over the floor. He doesn't know how to pick up after himself. Is this fair to his future wife? Could this have been corrected at home?

In the next chapter, we will look at discipline.

Chapter 11: Discipline

The greatest lesson you could teach your son is to be self-disciplined. The root word of discipline is disciple. The meaning of the word disciple is learner. Many educators tell me that the major problem with their students is not their math or reading scores but a lack of discipline.

My children's book, *A Culture of Respect,* evolved from a conversation I had with a principal who told me that her students did not respect each other or the teachers. Our boys lack home training. It is difficult to teach or learn without discipline. We have 18 years to develop discipline in our sons but are often unsuccessful. Parents are now sending their sons to the military as a last resort.

Is your son disciplined?

Does he respect authority?

Many mothers don't understand that although their sons give them respect, they are not respecting other adults. How many times have I heard, "I don't understand; he respects me." But that doesn't mean your son is disciplined. When your son is disciplined, he respects all adults.

Also, if your child only respects the belt, and schools cannot use the belt, we have a problem. There used to be a strong relationship between parents and neighbors, parents and teachers. We used to have a village, and children respected all adults.

As we mentioned earlier, there are two critical ages when your son is going to try you: 2 and 12. Are you ready for the showdown? The Bible is clear: when you spare the rod, you spoil the child (Proverbs 13:24). The rod may be successful when he's 2. For many boys of single mothers, the rod may not be as successful at age 12.

If the only thing your son respects is the belt, what are public schools to do since they are not allowed to use this form of punishment?

We often see discipline and punishment as one and the same. Punishment should be a "stage two" strategy, used only when your son has broken a rule. Discipline must be taught in "stage one."

The best way to teach is by example. It is difficult to tell your son not to smoke while you're smoking, not to drink while you're drinking, not to curse while you're cursing. It is difficult to encourage your child to read if he never sees you read.

Jesus taught his disciples by example.

There is no job more challenging than parenting, a 24/7 job that lasts a minimum of 18 years. Since our children are always watching us, we can best teach them by being good role models. Possibly one of the reasons why our boys are so resistant is because, especially in the African American community, they have no input in the rules that govern their lives. This is a touchy point because historically, Black parents have always believed in "Do it because I said so." There is some merit to that; in fact, this is exactly how it's done in the military. You do not question your superior. However, if we are serious about developing self-disciplined children, they need to have some input. That does not mean they can negotiate every point or that they will have the final decision. All I am saying is that before you make the final decision, let your son have his say. For example, let him suggest a time to do his chores.

Children want attention, especially boys who have large, insecure egos. Remember the class clown? Because of the large, insecure male ego, boys will either be your best or your worst students.

The only child faces unique discipline challenges. Given that he is the only child at home receiving all of the attention, he may have a difficult time sharing the teacher's time and attention with as many as 28 or 30 other students.

My grandson is an only child. He receives attention from his mother, father, grandparents, uncles, and aunts. He had to adjust to a very different experience in preschool.

Even negative attention from the teacher is better than no attention, so some boys act out. That is why it is so important to increase the praise you give your son. Let him know when he is doing things right, not just when he is being disobedient or misbehaving. If you want your son to be disciplined, *increase the praise*.

Discipline also needs goals to strive toward. When your son knows that he's expected to go to college, that he's going to be an engineer, that he will marry and *then* have children, discipline will carry him toward his goals.

However, if your son thinks he can stay in your house indefinitely, take six hours of college classes, and work ten hours a week at a fast food chain, he really doesn't need much discipline to get by.

Some mothers cannot believe their sons can be disciplined. They are shocked when, after a mere month in the military, their clothes are clean and pressed, they make their bed to perfection, and they are respectful to adults. They even get up early in the morning. I want someone to explain to me how the military can turn our sons around in 30 days when parents, who have 18 years, cannot get them to put out the garbage.

Many children lack discipline because we adults have been undisciplined in our personal lives. Our boys are living within a variety of family structures. Some of them live in homes where no one is married, and they are being reared by girlfriends, boyfriends, or fiancés. Mother has one rule and Daddy has another. Daddy has one rule and his girlfriend has another. Can you imagine how confusing this must be for children? Our children are not the problem; it's the adults in their lives.

Adults who are raising boys need to communicate and come to some consensus about what the rules are going to be. You can't have one household where the boy has to be in by 7:00 pm while the other household allows him to come in at midnight.

"Don't do as I do, but do as I say" doesn't work with children. We have to live by example. We can't be inconsistent with them.

Possibly the strongest reason boys reject our rules is negative peer pressure. The peer group is extremely important to boys, and peer pressure persuades them to do things they wouldn't ordinarily do. Black boys really value what their friends think of them. They often make critical decisions and mistakes because of what their peer group demands of them.

Too many of our boys are involved with gangs, drugs, and stealing because of negative peer pressure. They may have been raised in the best of homes, but they just can't resist the peer pressure.

In the face of peer pressure, boys must learn to weigh the consequences and benefits of their actions. They know that when they stay out late they are going to be punished, but staying out late means more at the moment than the consequences. Also, if parents do not consistently enforce punishment, they decide to test fate. Boys know that when you punish them, you punish yourself. They know that if they are going to be inside for three days, so are you, and this is why you may not have kept your word in the past.

When parents mete out punishments, they must be realistic. You can't tell your son that he's grounded for the rest of the year. That's unrealistic. You were hasty and angry when you said that, and now you're going to have to eat your words. That's why people should not spank their children when they're angry and irrational.

Let's talk about punishment. Now that the child has broken the rule in stage one, how do we respond in stage two? I recommend the following:

- Warning
- Time Out
- Denial
- The Belt

When your son breaks the rule, first give him a warning. Unfortunately, many mothers have overused warnings. Warnings should be used only one time. In basketball, if you get two technical fouls, you get thrown out. Same here. First technical foul is the warning. Your son will understand if you present it in a basketball context.

After one warning, put your son in time out. For some reason, parents with degrees and high incomes advocate time out while those with less education and money push for the belt. Each has its merits. Bottom line: parents need to be in agreement about their strategies.

It's not good for children when one parent believes in time out and the other believes in the belt. Also, if your son has a bachelor pad of a bedroom, telling him "time out, go to your room" may not be punishment. He should go to another part of the house for time out. The bedroom has too many toys for serious reflection.

Denial of an activity or privilege that he enjoys can be effective, but the punishment must fit the crime. It is unfair to deny your child Friday night basketball for the rest of the year when he was late only 15 minutes. There has to be fairness.

As a final resort, use the belt. As the boy's age increases, use of the belt should decrease. If you're going to use the belt, you need to be rational. Once with my son I combined both time out and the belt. I said, "Go to your room, and I'll be there in an hour to spank you." Within that hour he had "spanked" himself as he envisioned all that would be done to him. Not only did this help me with the punishment, but an hour later I was calm.

If you are going to use the belt, you should hit the buttocks with a proper object. The government has had to step in not because of the Bible's direction not to spare the rod but because people are slapping children in the face and hitting them with ironing cords and any object they can find. You don't throw books and bricks and glass at your children. You don't burn them with cigarettes. We're talking about a calm person using the right object on the right part of the body.

I know that some people are still not in favor of the belt, and we have the right to positively disagree. But please notice that the belt in my mind is a last resort. We recommend using many forms of discipline before we move to punishment, so the belt is not my first choice nor should it be used as our sons increase in age.

Anger

Our sons are having a difficult time managing their anger and developing self-control. Unfortunately, the world we live in is filled with violence. Making one mistake could cost them their lives.

When I was growing up, brushing up against someone or saying the wrong thing would lead to a disagreement or fistfight. But we lived to see another day. Today, if boys make one mistake, if they don't manage their anger, if they have no self-control, they could lose their lives.

How do we help our boys manage their anger?

How do we help our sons develop self-control?

We must teach our sons the difference between battles and wars. Sometimes it's better to lose the battle and be around for the war. Many of our boys have never been taught to say "my fault," "I'm sorry," or "my bad." These words could save their lives.

We've developed a course for schools called the Dr. King Class of Nonviolence, which teaches boys how to resolve conflict through nonviolence. Many of our boys have a chip on their shoulders. They're just waiting for someone to knock it off so they can fight. Ironically, what the angriest boy in the school really needs—the one who's 6' 3", wears size 16 gym shoes, and has a scowl on his face—is a hug.

We could soothe that anger out of him simply with a hug, a smile, and a word of encouragement. Ideally, he would receive that love from his parents, but as I mentioned before, a week may go by before he even speaks to his parents. Can you imagine a child going Monday through Friday and not speaking to his parents? We're not talking about how many words of encouragement he's received. He really doesn't care at that point. He just wants someone to talk to him. Unfortunately, the object of his anguish, his parent, is not even present. That's enough to make anyone angry.

Living in households with boyfriends and girlfriends, fiancés, and foster parents is enough to make a boy angry.

When a boy is being interviewed by his fourth potential adoptive parent, it's enough to make him angry.

Gangsta rap makes our boys angry.

Many of our boys are not being reared in reverence of the Lord. They do not understand the power of prayer, the Word, a Savior who said, "I'll never leave you or forsake you" (Hebrews 13:5). God made all of us empty, and he gave us free will. Many don't know they're angry because they do not know Christ as their personal Lord and Savior. They keep thinking it's something else, but until they give their lives to Christ, they will remain empty.

We need to teach our boys discipline through martial arts *before* sending them off to the military. I'm a strong advocate of martial arts. Boys can learn discipline and self-control through martial arts.

My book *Developing Positive Self-Images and Discipline in Black Children* has some comical statements which, unfortunately, can become a reality if we don't implement the above strategies.

1. Begin with infancy to give the child everything he wants. In this way he will grow up to believe the world owes him a living.

2. When he picks up bad words, laugh at him. This will make him think he's cute. It will also encourage him to pick up "cuter" phrases that will blow off the top of your head later.

3. Never give any spiritual training. Wait until he is 21 and then let him "decide for himself."

4. Avoid use of the word "wrong." It may develop a guilt complex. This will condition him to believe later, when he is arrested for stealing a car, that society is against him and he is being persecuted.

5. Pick up everything he leaves lying around —books, shoes, clothes. Do everything for him so that he will be experienced in throwing all responsibility on others.

6. Let him read any printed matter he can get his hands on. Be careful that the silverware and drinking glasses are sterilized, but let him mind feast on garbage.

7. Quarrel frequently in the presence of your children. In this way they will not be too shocked when the home is broken up later.
8. Give the child all the spending money he wants. Never let him earn his own. Why should he have things as tough as you had them?
9. Satisfy his every craving for food, drink, and comfort. See that every sensual desire is gratified. Denial may lead to harmful frustration.
10. Take his part against neighbors, teachers, policemen. They are all prejudiced against your child.
11. When he gets into real trouble, apologize for yourself by saying: "I never could do anything with him."
12. Never know where your child is or what he's doing when he's away from home.
13. Don't inquire into the background, personalities, records, and habits of the kids he particularly pals around with.
14. Prepare for a life of grief. You'll be likely to have it.

Chapter 12: Character

I know parents, mothers and fathers, who give their children so many toys they literally need to have another room just for storage. Instead of buying your children toys, spend time with them to develop their character. One of the most important gifts you can give your son is character. It's more important than money, gold, and silver. It transcends time. It can be developed no matter your economic circumstances. Character can never be taken away.

The following are characteristics of character:

- Dependability
- Manners
- Respect of elders
- Respect of women
- Truth
- Integrity
- Attitude
- Family pride
- Sharing
- Confidence
- Assertiveness
- Psychology of performance
- Work ethic
- Needs vs. wants
- Values

My name, Jawanza, means "dependable." I got it legally from my father. My father was the most dependable man I have ever known. He taught me that a man is only as strong as his word. If you have a strong word, if people can count on your word, you will never be broke. You can use your word as collateral because people will have confidence in your word. My father worked at the post office from 3:00 pm to 11:00 pm. He called my sister and me literally every night at 8:00 pm from ages 2 to 18 and never missed a night.

Let's teach our sons the value of their word.

In the movie *Domestic Disturbance,* the son of John Travolta's character lives with his mother and stepfather. The son tells Travolta that the stepfather is abusive. When queried by the police, Travolta says, "My son does not lie." The son's word was enough for Travolta to investigate the matter.

Imagine if we as parents could honestly and confidently say, "My son does not lie."

Can you confidently say your son does not lie?

The idea for my children's book *A Culture of Respect* came from the principal of a school. When asked about the major challenges facing her school she said, "We lack a culture of respect." Unfortunately, many of our boys lack home training. For 18 years their parents failed them, and it takes sending their sons to the military to get them to say things like:

- Yes, sir.
- No, sir.
- Yes, ma'am.
- No, ma'am.
- Good morning.
- Thank you.
- Please.
- I'm sorry.

These are critical words that everybody, especially our sons, need to know. It's unfortunate that many parents have placed the burden of home training on the school. Note the vernacular: it's called *home* training. Schools should not have to teach children *home* training.

You can tell a lot about a boy by his home training, his manners. Parents tell me that children with home training are always welcome in their homes, but children with no manners are too difficult to manage. The common denominator is home training and manners.

In African and most cultures, one of the ways you measure people is by how well they respect their elders. Does your son respect his elders? If your son was sitting on the bus and an elder got on, would he offer his seat if there were no other seats?

Your son is on the corner with his friends, and an elder walks by. Will your son acknowledge the elder? Will your son give the elder respect? If the boys are cursing among themselves, will they stop in the presence of the elder?

Will your son make elders feel safe as they walk by? A people are in trouble when elders are afraid of the children.

If we're going to be successful in developing character in our boys, we must teach them to respect females of all ages. In the chapter on sexuality, we will talk about how some males are so abusive and disrespectful to women that they have no problem running trains on them. We'll also deal with the fallout of Don Imus using the B and H words.

First, however, we must come to terms with whether your son respects females of all ages. Is it possible for a son to disrespect his mother and respect other females? Is it possible for a boy to have selective respect?

The same demon that drives racism drives sexism. Blacks and Whites are different, but it doesn't mean that Whites are better. Insecurity makes racists believe their differences make them better than others. Many Whites are insecure, so they convince themselves they are better than Blacks to boost their self-esteem. It's a mental illness.

The same thing applies to sexism. Men and women are different. One is not better than the other, just different. Insecure people will rationalize that their differences make them better.

We have a problem when African American men only see the speck of racism in the White man's eye but can't see the log of sexism in their own eyes. Sexism occurs when African American pastors refuse to allow women leadership roles in the church and when women are not allowed decision-making roles in civil rights and other organizations. Sexism occurs when men believe that maintaining the household is woman's work. This is not a good message to send our sons.

One of every three wives is physically abused. No telling how many wives are emotionally abused. Words are so powerful.

The demon that drives racism and sexism is power. Insecure people are obsessed with power.

Are you raising a sexist boy?

Are you raising a boy who does not respect women?

Are you raising a boy who believes he's superior to women?

Does your boy believe it is okay to physically and emotionally abuse women?

Are you raising a boy to view women as Bs and Hs?

Sixty-eight percent of our children are reared in households led by women, so if there's any issue that we have the power to resolve, it should be this one. Mothers should make absolutely sure their sons are not sexist.

Integrity

Have you taught your son to have integrity? This is an important virtue. If our boys can be taught to have integrity, they will be rich.

Integrity is what you do when no one is watching. It comes from within, not without.

Genesis 39 tells the story of Joseph. When Potiphar's wife tried to entice Joseph, he told her, "I can't do that." He could not disappoint God. This is integrity.

What do you do when no one is watching you? When Jesse Jackson, Sr., was a boy, his father had him work with him, cleaning up offices. The officer would always leave money on his desk to try and tempt them. Jesse's father said, "This will measure your integrity. Even if no one sees you taking the money, God will."

What do you do when no one is watching? Does your son have integrity?

One of the ways to measure character is by your attitude.

ATTITUDE

The longer I live, the more I realize the impact of attitude on life. Attitude, to me, is more important than actions. It is more important than the past, than education, than money, than circumstances, than failures, than successes, than what other people think or say or do. It is more important than appearance, giftedness, or skill.

The remarkable thing is we have a choice every day regarding the attitude we will embrace for that day. We cannot change our past, our neighborhood, family, income, or parents. We cannot change that fact that people will act in a certain way, that sometimes friends, parents, and teachers get on our nerves. The only thing we can do is play on the one string we have; and that is our attitude. **I am convinced that life is 10 percent what happens to us and 90 percent how we react to it.**

In my book *Sankofa: Stories of Power, Hope, and Joy* I share the story of a couple who had twins. On Christmas they gave one of their sons a room full of toys. Unfortunately, in less than a week most of the toys had been broken, and he was no longer interested in playing with the toys. This son had a bad attitude.

The other son received a room full of horse manure. Can you imagine, it's Christmas day. The child is expecting toys and other great gifts, but instead his room is full of horse manure.

If someone gave you a room full of horse manure, how would you feel?

This son had a positive attitude. He knew his parents loved him and that they wouldn't do him any harm. When he opened the door and saw all the horse manure he thought, "There's got to be a pony in here somewhere." He proceeded to dig through the manure and found a million-dollar pony.

Which son is yours? The first or the second?

Principals, teachers, coaches, and employers tell me that many of our males have a bad attitude. One of the ways we make a distinction between winners and losers is by their attitude. I'm reminded of the woman in the Bible who lost her only son. The prophet, the man of God, asked her, "Is everything well with you? Is everything well with your husband? Is everything well with your child?"

Her son was dead, but she said, "It is well." She didn't speak from a physical perspective. She spoke from the spirit realm. In less than 24 hours, the man of God healed her son. I believe the reason why her son lived was because of her attitude and her positive confession.

I love sports because they teach character. Take baseball. It's the ninth inning, and the other team is winning nine to zero. There are two outs, and our worst batter is at the plate. Two strikes are already against him, yet we have to believe we can win. It is still possible to win. Many times a team will come back from behind to win the game. Our boys need to learn this lesson.

Asian parents teach their children the importance of the family name and pride in family and community. They teach them an appreciation of their family tree. Asian children learn that they represent more than just themselves; they represent family.

This used to be an African principle, and it still is in some homes. The numbers are dwindling, however. We need to teach our children that they represent more than themselves. They represent the family. Our children must learn to appreciate their family heritage. Unfortunately, most can only go back one or two generations. It's one thing to protest the failure of schools to teach students African history, but how do we explain parents not teaching their own family history?

How far back can you and your children go in the family lineage? Who is the oldest member of your family? Visit that person and find out as much as you can because his or her days are numbered.

Teach your son to value his family name, to represent his family well.

The family is the first school a child will ever know, and it is here where he will learn how to share with others. Children are born selfish and self-centered. Ideally, as the child gets older, he becomes less self-centered and begins to share. As the age increases, self-centeredness should decrease. Unfortunately, that is not always the case.

Many adults are self-centered. My wife mentioned how people just love to talk on and on about themselves. This is a major attribute of males who seem to become more self-centered as time goes on.

Being a good listener will take you far in life. It's a good trait to have. The rumor is that women are better listeners than men. We must teach our sons to be more caring and less self-centered and to listen and value what others are experiencing. The world does not revolve around them.

A great joy in parenting comes when your son asks how *you* are doing and shows concern about *you.* When this occurs, you know you've done a good job in raising him.

I pray you are not raising a self-centered, selfish child.

I am involved in numerous rites of passage and mentoring programs. One exercise requires the boys to line up on one side of the room, the men on the other. The boys walk toward us and extend their hands for a handshake. They are expected to give us a firm handshake, to look us in the eye. Then, with good volume, they tell us their names and a little bit about themselves. You can tell a lot about a man by his handshake. Confident people have a firm handshake and make excellent eye contact. They do not mumble; they project well.

How firm is your son's handshake?

Does he make excellent eye contact when speaking to someone?

Does your son project his voice well?

These behaviors are indicators of confidence.

We need to teach our sons the distinction between being assertive, passive, and aggressive. Many males are aggressive.

Our boys walk into school with a chip on their shoulders. They are angry, mad, and they want someone, whether it's a child or an adult, to knock the chip off their shoulder so they can verbally or physically abuse them. We must do everything we can to teach boys more effective ways to communicate. We must help them take the chip off their shoulders.

With our boys having only 7 minutes at best with fathers and 34 minutes with mothers, they need more time and TLC, tender loving care.

At the other extreme are the boys who are weak and passive. While some parents are developing thugs, others are developing sissies. These boys always accept what people say. They suck it up. They don't express their feelings. Just as we must help males work through their aggressive tendencies, we must help passive, weak males to "man up."

Aggression and passivity both indicate a lack of balance, and it is our job to help boys understand that true manhood is multidimensional. Through maturity and wisdom, a man balances strength, courage, tenderness, and the warrior instinct within him.

Let us teach our sons to be assertive. Assertive men are respectful in their disagreements. They let it be known in a positive way what they think and how they feel. It is important for parents to encourage their sons to speak up and express their feelings, but in a respectful way.

It is also important to teach boys how to win. There really is a psychology of performance. Jeff Howard of the Efficacy Committee in Massachusetts has done great work in the psychology of performance. Believe it or not, sports are more mental than physical, and there are certain traits that winners and losers possess. The four components of the psychology of performance are:

1. Ability
2. Effort
3. Luck
4. The nature of the task

People with strong self-esteem attribute their success to their ability and effort. If they do well on a math test, they believe their success was due to ability and studying hard. When winners fail a test, they never question their ability. They believe they just need to study harder. Character is developed when after failing a project, you try again because self-esteem says, "I can do this." On the next attempt, you succeed and learn a great lesson for the next time. That's how winners think.

Students who lack self-esteem and have not been taught the psychology of performance have not learned how to turn failure into success. When they do well on a math test, they attribute it to luck or the simplicity of the task. Consequently, when they do poorly on a test, they attribute it to their lack of ability, which means there's no need to study harder.

Helping our boys understand how to apply the psychology of performance to everything they do will take them far in life. As long as they know that their effort can transform failure into success, they will always be in control.

Work Ethic

Work ethic may be the most important component of this chapter. Does your son have a good work ethic?

Before God gave Eve to Adam , God gave Adam a job. He was responsible for naming the animals. He was a zoologist. In 2 Thessalonians 3:10, the Bible says, "If a man does not work, a man does not eat."

Jean Lush's excellent book, *Mothers and Sons,* makes the following observations:

For many years, as a family therapist, I consulted numerous unemployed men with families. It was routine for me to explore their backgrounds. Despite many job opportunities, these men couldn't hold a job. Even when they liked a particular kind of work, inevitably something went wrong and they were unemployed again. *In all these cases I consistently saw one common denominator: these men were never required to work around the house when they were growing up. They were never taught to responsibly and efficiently complete a chore.[4]*

Jean Lush's observation is so insightful. We could crack the code here. Parents, you can improve your son's work ethic simply by giving him chores to do.

In a CNN documentary, a Black employer with a multi-million-dollar landscaping company said he used to hire Black employees but he became so frustrated with their poor attendance and performance that he began hiring Hispanics. Can you imagine, a Black employer says that Hispanic workers have a better work ethic than his own people! Is that true?

Why were Africans brought to this country? The rumor is that we are lazy. If we were so lazy, why didn't Whites work themselves? Why did they travel three months on a slave ship to get a lazy people and another three months to bring us back to America to work? What happened to our work ethic?

Men my age love talking about the good old days when as young as 9 and 10 years old we had paper routes. Our paper routes helped develop our work ethic. To be 9 years old and have to get up at 5:00 in the morning, in the cold, to deliver 100 papers takes a tremendous commitment. When a boy does that at 9, the sky is the limit on what he will do as an adult. Unfortunately, our neighborhoods are no longer safe enough for children to deliver newspapers. Those jobs are now being done by adults.

Today, many boys only choose between doing lawn work and being the lookout for crack dealers. Sadly, no industry pays better than crack cocaine.

Is there a relationship between chores and work ethic? Is there a relationship between how well your son does his chores and his job performance? Is there a relationship between boys getting up early and, as adults, getting to work on time? Jean Lush hit the nail on the head with her significant observation.

Are you raising a lazy male?

Are you raising a male who can't keep a job?

Are you raising a male who cannot perform a job satisfactorily?

How well does your son do chores?

Does your son have to do chores at all?

I never liked letting my sons sleep late in the morning during spring breaks and summer vacations. There was something about it that just irritated me. They were too young to stay in bed until noon. There are households where boys sleep until noon, wake up, look for something to eat, watch television, listen to music, play video games, and then at 5:00 or 6:00 in the afternoon, go outside, hang on the corners until midnight, come home to sleep again from midnight to noon, and then repeat the process the next day.

I mentioned earlier that my wife would inspect our sons' work at home like a military sergeant, and if their chores weren't done well they couldn't go out and play. It was not enough for them to do their chores. How well they did their chores will tell you how well they will work as employees.

I am aware of institutional racism and how African Americans are denied jobs based on race. I am also aware that African Americans often perform the same jobs as Whites but are paid less. Certain issues are systemic and external but others are internal, and one should not negate the other.

Historically, in the Black community, there has been a debate between the Integrationists and the Nationalists, Douglass and Delany, Booker T. Washington and DuBois, DuBois and Garvey, King and Malcolm, Jesse Jackson and Louis Farrakhan. In essence, the debate boils down to whether we emphasize racism or personal effort in assessing our progress as a people. You can decide for yourself to what extent racism impacts the problem, but I believe we ourselves will have to be 90 percent or more of the solution to our problems. I've devoted my career to looking for solutions.

As a former track runner (the 1600 meter relay), I was often the anchor on the relay team. If we were 20 or 30 yards behind, I really didn't need to complain about why I was put in this situation. What I needed to do was get the baton and run the best race of my life—and win!

We spend too much time looking at why we are 20 and 30 yards behind when we need to focus on the road ahead. We have the ability to do that. One of the ways we can win the race is by developing excellence in everything we do. Teach your sons to get up early, do their chores well, and be punctual. Not only does this develop character but these are excellent business habits.

A particular employee of mine was consistently late. His starting time was 9:00 am but he would arrive around 9:20 or 9:30. I called him into my office and asked him to explain why he couldn't come to work on time. I told him this was unacceptable. Just as our children think being smart is acting White, this brother told me I was acting like the White man. He actually had the nerve to play the race card with me. If expecting our employees to be on time is acting White, something is seriously wrong with our values and our character. This employee probably grew up in a household where he was never taught to be on time and was allowed to sleep as long as he wanted.

Parents, you are laying the foundation for how your sons will behave as adults. We cannot expect that our sons, who have been irresponsible for 18 years, will magically become responsible at age 19. That is incomprehensible.

Needs vs. Wants

Does your son know the difference between a need and a want? He needs to learn the difference. Our children are lured to the crack business because they have not learned the difference between needing and wanting the things they see in commercials, billboards, and the *Lifestyles of the Rich and Famous*. They have decided they *need* a $150 pair of gym shoes. They *need* a $200 starter jacket. They *need* the latest hip-hop fashion wear. In many low-income neighborhoods, there are often more luxury cars and big-screen televisions than in affluent suburbs.

We must teach our sons early that the car note cannot exceed the rent or the mortgage. They must learn to live within their means, to understand the power of budgeting. You can't make $1,000, spend $1,500, and expect to be wealthy. Parents, if you have not learned this lesson, it will be difficult to teach your children.

My two sons wanted the latest pair of new gym shoes—the gym shoes that are made in South Korea for $2.38 and sold to our youth for $119.95. These are the gym shoes our boys will kill you over, for $2.38. I commend Stephon Marbury, the brilliant guard for the New York Knicks, who decided that if his shoes only cost $2.38 to make, he would sell them for $14.95.

I played the game of needs vs. wants with my sons. They did need a new pair of good gym shoes. I told them their mother and I would provide the money for the shoes, around $60. If they wanted to do extra chores or get a part time job to pay for a more expensive pair, they could do that. I wasn't against them having something they wanted, but I refused to buy it for them if it was an unnecessary want. My job was to take care of their needs. We must teach our boys the difference between needs and wants with everything—gym shoes, jackets, pants, suits, toys. Teach them what the needs cost and what the wants cost. The parent pays for the need, and the child pays for the want. This teaches self-discipline and builds character.

I can hear the boys now: "That's not fair!" Life is not fair. The question is, how is your son going to handle it? He'll get over the gym shoes, but what about more difficult issues, like discrimination and racism? These are difficult challenges for African Americans.

Children innately believe that life should be fair. As long as you play by one set of rules, then children are comfortable with that. Children are confused when mother has one rule and daddy has another. They are confused by "Don't do as I do, but do as I say." Children respond better when there is consistency and order.

Children don't understand why the teacher punishes them for hitting when all they were doing was hitting the child back who hit them first. The child who gets caught gets punished, not the one who started it in the first place. Same thing in basketball. The referee did not see the person who fouled you, but he did see you commit a retaliatory foul. That's not fair, and children don't understand that.

We must teach our children that life is not fair.

A Black man and a White man are doing the same job, but the White man receives a higher salary.

White students are called on more in class than Black students.

Parents, teach your sons that life is not fair without breaking their spirit. How do we keep that glow in our sons' eyes? How do we keep them innocent, curious, and still believing they can reach their full potential?

This is a difficult lesson to teach, but I provide the answer in the chapter on spirituality. The teacher and referee did not see the first infractions, but God did. If our boys believe in God, God will take care of them. God is the final judge. Vengeance belongs to Him. It is not necessary for our boys to take the law into their own hands.

Values

Maulana Karenga, the founder of the Nguzo Saba and Kwanzaa, says our struggle is not over materialism. It is about values. Below is the Nguzo Saba:

- Unity
- Self-Determination
- Collective Work and Responsibility
- Cooperative Economics
- Purpose
- Creativity
- Faith

Many books list these principles. We pull them out for seven days in December during Kwanzaa and then put them away until next year. This also happens during Black History Month; schools pull out the famous Black leaders for 28 days and then put them away.

Parents, if you are serious about teaching your son character and values, hang a poster listing the Nguzo Saba in his room, and frequently remind him about the principles.

The following are ways the Nguzo Saba can be used in the rearing of our boys.

Unity. Tell your son there will be no strife in the home. He will get along with his siblings and parents. He will respect his parents. The family needs to be unified.

When I was a boy, I was close to a family of brothers. The mother told her oldest son, "You're closer to Jawanza than your brothers. You need to defend your brothers." We must use every possible example to teach our sons the importance of unity.

Self-Determination. From this day on, do not allow the word "can't" to be spoken in your home. Philippians 4:13 says, "I can do all things through Christ who strengthens me." We must convince and teach our sons that they can do anything. They can excel in science, math, and reading as well as sports, music, and rap. The sky is the limit on their potential.

Collective Work and Responsibility. In addition to doing chores, there will be times when the entire family must work together to help get things done. Everyone must help one another. If a gathering is taking place at the house, we are all responsible for cleaning and getting the entire house ready. When your son finishes his own chores, then he is to reach out and help someone else.

Cooperative Economics. Teach your son how to develop a budget. Start him early with his allowance. Teach him the importance of tithing and saving.

Purpose. We must help our sons develop goals. They should be able to provide a different career for each letter of the alphabet. Our boys make mistakes when they have nothing to lose. They are not at risk because they're low income or from a single-parent family. They are at risk when they lack goals and a purpose in life.

Creativity. You can tell an awful lot about your son by looking at his room. What kinds of images are in your son's room?

Faith. More will be said about faith in the chapter on spirituality.

In the next three chapters, we will look chronologically at the growth and development of our sons. First, we will look at the preschool years.

Chapter 13: Preschool Years

There are three critical grades: kindergarten, fourth grade, and ninth grade. If you want to see God at His best, look at our boys in kindergarten. If you want to see Satan at his best, look at our boys in ninth grade.

I speak at many conferences on school readiness, where I make my criticisms of K–12 educators known. However, the preschool years are primarily the responsibility of parents. When children enroll in kindergarten, they should be academically and socially prepared to learn. Often this is not the case. Parents need to do better in preparing their children for school.

Children possess a quality that is essential to achieving their dreams: they know no limits. They do not know what they cannot do, so they dream big dreams. They are limited only by their imagination. An interesting study found that few adults can be classified as highly creative; however, 95 percent of all 4-year-olds studied were considered creative. Unfortunately, only 4 percent of all 7-year-olds studied retained their creativity. What happened to these children? The answer is obvious: they entered kindergarten and began to learn what they could not do.

We must do everything we can to retain our children's creativity, their innocence, the glow in their eyes.

The first years in a child's life are critical. Fifty percent of the brain is developed in the first six months. Eighty percent of the brain is developed during the first three years. It is criminal for a child to grow up in a house full of smoke, poor diet, inappropriate music, and unlimited amounts of television viewing. Parents, we must be at our best during their first three years.

In the ridiculous book *The Bell Curve*, Charles Murray attempted to document that African children are genetically inferior to White children. He used IQ tests to make his case, but do these tests measure innate intelligence (nature, genetics) or exposure (nurture)?

To compare the innate intelligence of Black and White children, do not look at the results of tests taken in the eighth and twelfth grades. By then, students have been exposed to years of education, and it is difficult to attribute test results to innate intelligence or exposure. In addition, the tests used to determine our children's intelligence are, without a doubt, culturally biased.

What was Washington's first name? From a White perspective, the answer is George. From a Black perspective, the answer might be Booker T. or Harold (Chicago's first Black mayor).

What color is a banana? In affluent neighborhoods, bananas are yellow and green. In poor communities, bananas are brown.

Charles Murray, the earlier you test and compare children the better. The excellent book written by the late scholar Amos Wilson, *The Developmental Psychology of the Black Child,* offers the following:

Comparison of African-European Psychomotor Development	
9 hours old	Is drawn up into a sitting position. Able to prevent the head from falling backwards (European child, 6 weeks).
2 days old	With head held firmly, looks at face of the examiner (European child, 8 weeks).
7 weeks old	Supports himself in a sitting position and watches his reflection in the mirror (European child, 20 weeks).
5 months old	Holds himself upright (European child, 9 months) and takes the round blocks out of their holes in the foam board (European child, 9 months).
5 months old	Stands against the mirror (European child, 9 months).
7 months old	Walks to the gazelle box to look inside (European child, 18 months).
11 months old	Climbs the steps along (European child, 15 months).

It is not my desire to compare children of various races, but we live in such a racist society, where African Americans are constantly put on the defensive by ill-prepared writers like Charles Murray, that I wanted to put this genetic argument to rest. Our children our suffering because of a lack of exposure, tracking, and low expectations. They are not genetically inferior.

Parents, during the preschool years it is critical that every day, every moment becomes a learning experience. Give your sons every opportunity to learn so that they will reach their full potential. With each passing year, nurturing becomes more and more important.

Nutritional Risk Factors

With 50 percent of the brain being developed in the first six months and 80 percent in the first three years, your son must have nutritional foods to fuel that growth. Foods and liquids that contain chemicals and sugar should be reduced or eliminated.

You may have been raised to believe that children need cow's milk to develop their brains and bodies, but as you'll read in this section, nothing could be further from the truth. This is a lie that the dairy industry has been spreading since the 1950s, with help from the USDA (U.S. Department of Agriculture), doctors, and celebrities (including, ironically, lactose-intolerant Whoopi Goldberg).

Mother's milk is God's food for infants. Only 19 percent of African American mothers breastfeed their children. God provides a mother the milk she needs to nourish her child. Milk is not to be consumed by adults for the rest of their lives.

God did not intend for puppies to drink cat's milk, nor did he design or desire human babies to drink cow's milk.

All milk is not the same.

In my book *Satan, I'm Taking Back My Health* the following description of milk is provided:

FACTOR	HUMAN	COW
Casein percentage	50%	82%
Whey percentage	60%	18%
Calcium-Phosphoric	Ratio 2 to 1	Ratio 1.2 to 1
Vitamin A per liter	1898mg.	1028 mg.
Niacin per liter	1470mg.	940mg.
Vitamin C per liter	43mg.	11mg.
Reaction in the body:	Alkaline	Acidic

COMPARISON OF THE MILKS OF DIFFERENT SPECIES

	Mean values for protein content per cent.	Time required to double birth weight (days)
HUMAN	1·2	180
MARE	2·4	60
COW	3·3	47
GOAT	4·1	19
DOG	7·1	8
CAT	9·5	7
RAT	11·8	4·5

Cow's milk accelerates development of the body; mother's milk develops the brain. One of the consequences of children drinking cow's milk is precocious puberty, the onset of puberty before its time. Girls have been starting their menstrual cycles, on average, six months earlier every decade since 1930. We have little girls as young as 8 years old who have started their cycle and are able to give birth to a child. Children who are given cow's milk are growing like cows and not like humans.

I'm pleading with mothers: breastfeed your son. Mother's milk is not only the best food for your son's brain but breastfeeding creates a bond between mother and son that is indescribable.

Ironically, the country—the United States—that consumes the most milk has the highest incidence of osteoporosis. The dairy industry promotes the idea that osteoporosis is caused by a calcium deficiency, which can be remedied by consuming more milk. But we already consume more than any other nation. Obviously, this may not be the solution to the problem.

The real culprit is the acidity created by the large amounts of meat Americans consume. The body's attempt to balance acid draws upon calcium stores, creating an alkaline affect.

After you wean your son from the breast, replace your milk not with cow's milk but with soy, sesame, or coconut milk.

From Home to Preschool

Many female teachers have designed a female classroom for large numbers of male students. As a result, African American boys are placed in special education four times as often as African American girls and White boys two times as often as White girls. But boys and girls really are different.

One of the things we've noticed about boys in the preschool years is the tremendous attachment they have to their parents, especially their mothers. Research has shown that boys are affected more by abandonment and separation from their parents, particularly their mothers. It is unfortunate that our economy requires mothers to drop off their infants, babies, and toddlers at the preschool center. Boys are affected by this more than girls.

One of my employees was pregnant, and she already had two sons. The budget was tight, but she and her husband decided that it was important for her to stay home and raise the three boys. I really respected that. They clearly understood the distinction between needs and wants.

If we must place our children in preschool programs at such an early age, we need to do everything possible to ease this traumatic transition. Mothers, if possible, go to the preschool to breastfeed and visit your son. This is the most important period in your son's life, and it must be taken seriously.

Age Two

We should not call this age the Terrible Two's. Remember the power of words. Let us call this age the Wonderful Two's or Terrific Two's. Boys will challenge their parents at the age of 2. Can you imagine, there are parents who cannot handle a 2-year-old challenging them. If you can't handle him at 2, heaven forbid what will happen at age 12. You must be ready to deal effectively with your son when he begins to challenge you at age 2.

There are gender differences in attention span, energy level, verbal skills, hearing skills, fine motor development, and gross motor development. One of the most important areas is maturation. Girls mature faster than boys. Europe understands this and adjustments have been made. What is so magical about all children going to full day kindergarten at age 5? Many boys are not yet ready for kindergarten at age 5. Europe allows their boys to start kindergarten at age 6. We will later look at the fact that many boys are failing kindergarten because they are not emotionally ready.

In addition to providing our children with a nurturing environment, nutritious food, and breast milk, at this critical period, the preschool years, we must realize the importance of our words. Remember the power of encouraging and discouraging words. In some homes, regardless of income, children receive 500,000 encouragements by the age of 3 and only 80,000 discouragements. In other homes, this age group receives only 75,000 encouragements and more than 200,000 discouragements.

If we are serious about these preschool years, every effort should be made to reduce discouragements and increase encouragements. Often, before our boys even get to kindergarten, their spirits have been broken by our discouragements. Even the 80,000 discouragements are excessive.

Parents, when your son does something wrong, criticize his behavior, not him as a person. Do not break his spirit; do everything you can to maintain his self-esteem.

During the preschool years, we must develop our children's vocabulary. It hurts me when I ask a kindergarten boy, "What's your name?" and he tells me "Boo" or "Bebe." Five years old and he still doesn't know his full name, his parents' names, his address, telephone number, age, letters, and numbers. Parents, refer to your son by his name, not a nickname. The nickname is not his name.

Some families speak volumes of words to their children. Your son's vocabulary is an indicator of his readiness for school. During the preschool years, we must speak to our children, and we must listen to them. We must help them grow their vocabulary. Every day we ourselves should learn a new word.

Some children by age 3 have a vocabulary of 1,100 words. Unfortunately, other children only have 525 words in their vocabulary. We cannot blame this academic deficiency on schools. Whatever deficiency we see at this age is the result of what's going on at home.

Besides talking to them, the most effective way to increase our boys' vocabulary is by reading to them. In some homes, by age 3, the child has received more than 20,000 hours of literacy. Some parents have told me they read to their child in the womb. Before their son even came into the world, the mother was reading to him. If they read to them in the womb, imagine how they will do years later.

Unfortunately, some children enter kindergarten without ever having had a book read to them. They do not appreciate the reading and storytelling experience. I appeal to every parent: before your son goes to sleep, read him a story. It's not only excellent for bonding and improving the attention span but it stimulates a great appreciation for reading and expands the vocabulary. Reading stimulates the imagination, the fountainhead of creativity.

Ben Carson once told me that reading gave him a whole new view of the world. He could go via a book to places he had never been to. We must expand our children's horizons.

Parents, have you exposed your son to video games and television instead of books? Some boys have experienced 20,000 hours of reading while others have experienced 20,000 hours of video games and TV. That's why people like Charles Murray feel confident negatively comparing our children to Whites, no matter how unfair. In reality, he didn't compare intelligence; he compared children's exposure to literacy.

I hold parents personally responsible for their sons' lack of exposure to books. We cannot blame this on the White man. I have never met a White man who could force us to turn on the television and keep it on for 20,000 hours between infancy and age 5.

Toys vs. Tools

There is a difference between a toy and a tool. The worst toy you could ever buy your son is one that is already put together. Our children are so creative. If you buy them a toy that is put together, they are not motivated to do anything creative with the toy. Provide children with toys that they can take apart, study the parts, and then put back together, maybe in a different way, maybe better than the manufacturer even intended.

Buy toys that have academic benefits. Your child's toys should develop literacy, letters, numbers, fine motor skills, and gross motor skills.

While observing parents and children in toy stores, I am reminded of what happens at the dinner table when a 2-year-old refuses to eat his greens. Given a choice, he will not want a toy that teaches him letters and numbers. He wants a gun. Parents acquiesce and give children dessert instead of broccoli, guns instead of academic tools. This will come back to haunt you if you don't assert yourself during the preschool years.

The challenges facing our boys begin early. Studies conducted by Yale University and the Foundation for Child Development report that preschool students are expelled three times more often than K–12 students. The study found that 4-year-olds were expelled 1.5 times more often than 3-year-olds. Boys were expelled 4.5 times more often than girls. African Americans attending state-funded pre-kindergarten were twice as likely to be expelled as Latino and Caucasian children and more than five times as likely to be expelled as Asian American children. The pre-kindergarten expulsion rate was 6.7 per 1,000 pre-kindergarteners enrolled. Based on current enrollment rates, an estimated 5,117 pre-kindergarten children across the nation are expelled each year. This rate is 3.2 times higher than the national rate of expulsions for K–12 students, which is 2.1 per 1,000 enrolled. Four-year-olds were expelled about 50 percent more often than 3-year-olds.[5]

Can you imagine, more than 5,000 children are expelled from preschool. In a later chapter we will discuss the relationship between the schoolhouse track and the jailhouse track. Unfortunately, this track seems to begin before kindergarten. Ninety percent of all children expelled are male, and 99 percent of all preschool teachers are female. I would encourage you to visit preschool programs before you place your son.

Do not let any institution break your son's spirit. In many preschool programs, as early as 2, 3, and 4 years of age the boys are called "bad" and "troublemakers." They're placed in the corner.

Parents, do not tell your son he is a "bad boy." If preschools and parents are calling boys bad at 2, what are they going to be called at age 12?

College students say the reason they do not want to teach is because the children are too bad. If they are considered bad by African American adults, I wonder what White females think of our boys. We must remove this stigma that is connected to our boys.

In the next chapter, we will look at the wide array of schools. Not every boy is receiving the same educational experience. We must make sure that we choose the right environment for our children. It starts with preschool. Not every day care, preschool, or Head Start program is the same. It is crucial that parents realize the significance of the preschool years. Your son needs to be in a nurturing and academically stimulating environment, first at home and then in preschool.

Chapter 14: Schools

Your son's number-one job is to be a student, and he needs to know that. Don't let it become a cliché. When he comes home from school, he changes his clothes, eats a snack, then does his homework.

Your son needs to understand that he is a student first, not an athlete. I appreciate schools that have a "no pass, no play" policy. Students must have a certain GPA in order to play their sport. This rightly places the priority on academics, not sports.

If your son wants to work after school, let your policy be "no pass, no work." He cannot work if he has a poor GPA.

Surveys have discovered that many students, especially African Americans, are doing their homework late in the evening. Your son's priority is school, so he should not wait until late in the evening to do his homework.

Here's another poster for your son's room: "My job is to be a student."

Homeschool

Public school is not the only game in town. Parents can choose from among a variety of educational options, including homeschooling. I am a strong advocate of homeschooling. An excellent book that details one family's homeschooling experience is Paula Nabrit's *Morning By Morning: How I Homeschooled My Sons to Ivy League Colleges.*

Homeschooling is not just for the rich and famous or parents with graduate degrees. More than 100,000 African Americans are being homeschooled, and the numbers have been growing over the past decades. I love it when parents take their children's education into their own hands.

Single parents can also homeschool. Remember, you may be a single parent, but that doesn't mean you have to parent by yourself. I know of one single working mother who homeschooled her son up until the eighth grade. If you are committed to the process, God will help you every step of the way.

If you work from home and have a flexible schedule, homeschool is ideal. Working the late shift may also work. For example, if you work from 3:00 pm to 11:00 pm, you can find time to educate your son between 7:00 am and 2:00 pm. Your mate, grandparents, or someone else can take care of your child when you're at work. There are a myriad of possibilities that allow homeschool to work.

Nabrit says you don't have to have advanced degrees to homeschool your child. Obviously it is easier to homeschool children in the earlier grades, although I know parents who homeschooled their children K–12. Once you establish a routine, the process takes on a life of its own. Your job is to manage the experience for your child. If you do not feel comfortable teaching your first-grade son addition or letter recognition, you can bring in different people to help.

My company, African American Images, provides a homeschool curriculum—SETCLAE (Self-Esteem Through Culture Leads to Academic Excellence). As the homeschool purchasing agent, you buy the books, software, supplies, and supplemental texts and items needed for your child's lessons. You can hire a tutor to help you teach subjects you're uncomfortable with. If you're uncomfortable teaching fractions or decimals, you can invite a college student or another skilled person to tutor your child.

Take your son to the museum to learn science and technology. For physical education, take him to the health club or enroll him in park district programs in martial arts and yoga. For music appreciation, your city might offer free concerts at the downtown cultural center. Or have him sing in your church's choir. In addition to teaching songs, many youth music ministries teach music theory, vocalization techniques, and even instrument instruction.

For history and science projects, your student can watch the History Channel and the Discovery Channel. There are numerous channels on television that are geared to assist the homeschool parent.

The greatest challenge of homeschooling is the socialization factor. Put your son in a basketball league and martial arts classes so he is around other children in various settings, not just academic.

The ideal student-teacher ratio in a traditional school is 17:1. Unfortunately, many of our boys are in classrooms where the ratio is 34:1. Seventeen may be better than 34, but nothing is better than 1:1 (or one to whatever number of children are in your home).

I strongly recommend that you consider raising your boys in a homeschool environment. Not only will you be his best teacher but you can provide him with the nurturance boys need. You'll be protecting your son's spirit, and he'll grow up in a stimulating atmosphere of learning.

Christian Schools

If values, character, and spirituality are important in rearing boys, then we need to practice what we preach and enroll our children in a Christian school. It is unfortunate that we have taken the Bible and prayer out of schools and replaced them with metal detectors and security guards. If we are serious about protecting our sons' spirits, we must consider placing them in a Christian environment.

Boys need to know that whenever they have a challenge in school, they can pray about it and ask the Holy Spirit to give them the answer.

African Centered Schools

My book *An African Centered Response to Ruby Payne's Poverty Theory* discusses the benefits of an African centered education in much more detail that I can cover in this book. If you are considering this approach for your son, I would strongly suggest purchasing this book.

Black boys need to know their history. They need to be in an environment where Black history is taught throughout the year, not just in February. Children who know that Imhotep, not Hippocrates, was the first doctor do not associate being smart with acting White.

Our children associate being smart with being White when they are taught a Eurocentric curriculum. Many of our boys are suffering from post-traumatic slavery disorder. They are angry, and they fight and kill each other because they hate themselves. All this can be corrected in an African centered school.

In *An African Centered Response to Ruby Payne's Poverty Theory*, you'll read about schools that struggled with children at the 30th percentile on the state exam. When an African centered curriculum was implemented, the test scores improved to the 70th percentile, despite the fact that the test was still Eurocentric (culturally biased).

When children are taught their history and culture, they become more confident in all subjects, especially math and science.

Single Gender Schools

An all male school would be an excellent option for your son. I am very pleased with the growth of single gender schools. Anyone who has followed my career knows that I began advocating for single gender schools in 1985. I spoke at the National Association of Black School Educators (NABSE) convention in 1985, and I recommended single gender schools and classrooms.

It has been a three-decade fight, but finally the government has agreed to implement single gender schools. The change occurred not because of the needs of the African American community but because NOW (National Organization of Women) and feminists grew frustrated at the injustice and inconsistency of White girls outperforming White boys K–12 but underperforming in the professional ranks. In other words, White females have found that when females study by themselves, not only do they improve academically but they become more confident in math and science.

I am pleased with the growth of single gender schools. One of the reasons why so many boys are placed in special education is because teachers do not allow for gender differences. With single gender schools, we can't help but allow for those differences. There was never anything wrong with our boys. Boys are simply different from girls.

I encourage you to read my books *Countering the Conspiracy to Destroy Black Boys* and *Keeping Black Boys Out of Special Education.* Also, visit the website of the National Association of Single Sex Public Education to learn about this tremendous movement.

Ideally, we would like to have Black male teachers teach Black male students, but there are two major problems. First, only 1 percent of America's teachers are African American males. Second, the unions. If we thought we had a problem implementing single gender classrooms in schools, we'd have a major problem if we required that single gender classrooms had to be taught by the same gender teacher.

I am willing to compromise on the gender of the teacher to secure a single gender classroom. In my book *Black Students / Middle Class Teachers* I document that it's not the race or gender of the teacher but the expectations and classroom management skills of the teacher that make the difference. I would love to have a Black male teacher teach African American male students, but if the African American male teacher has low expectations, poor classroom management skills, and requires little time on task, then he will be of no help to our boys. However, if a White female teacher has high expectations, good classroom management skills, and understands the importance of time on task, I'm willing to go with the White female teacher.

I would encourage you to visit some single gender schools, especially the Eagles Academy in the Bronx in New York City. There's a lot to love about the Eagles Academy. Not only does the school provide a single gender experience, a nurturing environment, and high expectations but it is led by one of the best principals in the country, David Banks. Also, every male student is paired with a mentor. I cannot stress enough that Black boys must have mentors.

Kipp Academy

I am an advocate of Kipp because I value greater time on task. The Kipp Academy understands that neither race, gender, income level, nor parental involvement or education are the most important factors in successful education. The most important variable is time on task.

Kipp Academy has a longer school day than most schools: eight hours rather than six during the week, four hours on Saturday. And summer vacation lasts only six weeks. The results have been phenomenal. These Black and Hispanic children from low income, single-parent homes are at the highest quartile. Kipp understands the importance of time on task.

When you close schools for three months during the summer, research shows that 80 percent of what your child learned during the school year will be lost if not properly reinforced during the summer.

We may not have a racial achievement gap. We may have a summer learning gap. White parents often send their children to academic and learning enrichment camps during the summer. Some travel the world. Our Black children, on the other hand, are playing basketball and watching rap videos for three months.

Some schools eliminate the summer learning gap by keeping it open year round with four three-week vacations throughout the year. This is a creative way of improving time on task.

Montessori Schools

I endorse Montessori because, due to nurture (not nature), many African American children are right-brain, hands-on learners. Right-brain learners perform better with oral lesson plans, pictures, music, and hands-on-activities. Left-brain learners perform better with textbooks, ditto sheets, and learning in the abstract. Unfortunately, many schools are left-brain oriented even though they have right-brain-thinking children. Many schools believe that the ideal student is the one who can sit still for long periods of time, quietly working on ditto sheets that lie about Columbus discovering America.

116

As an educational consultant to schools, I have also noticed that the math achievement gap is wider than the reading gap. The reason for this is that we have left-brain, abstract-thinking teachers working with right-brain, concrete-thinking students.

Montessori understands the split-brain theory. There are at least five ways to learn: written, oral, pictures, fine arts, and artifacts. Black children often do better K–3 than 4–12 because K–3 uses a whole-brain pedagogy. All five formats are used. A left-brain format is used with right-brain-thinking children starting in fourth grade. Montessori emphasizes a whole-brain pedagogy, right-brain learning styles, and more movement in the classroom.

High Achieving Public Schools

There are hundreds of schools in low-income Black neighborhoods that are high achieving. These schools have several similar traits, including administrators who do not see themselves as the CEO of the building. They see themselves as instructional leaders. I encourage you to place your son in a school where the principal spends very little time in the office. The bulk of the school day is spent visiting and monitoring teachers.

High achieving schools are aware that teachers are not the same. There are five types of teachers: custodians, referral agents, instructors, teachers, and coaches.

Low achieving schools have a large number of custodians. These are teachers who say, "I have mine and you have yours to get" and "I have one year, four months, three weeks, two days, and I'm retired." Basically, they are babysitters.

Referral agents do not teach. They refer students to special education and suspension. Research shows that 20 percent of the teachers are making 80 percent of the referrals to special education and suspension.

From the fourth grade on, there are many instructors. These educators believe they teach subjects, not children. For many Black and Latino children, there can be no significant learning until we first establish a significant relationship. ***Two consecutive years of an ineffective teacher could destroy your son for life.*** Parents, do everything possible to make sure your son doesn't spend one extra day with a custodian, referral agent, or instructor. If you have to take your son out of that school and take him home, to your office, to another school, do whatever it takes to save your son. I cannot imagine how many custodians, referral agents, and instructors have destroyed our sons.

The only two kinds of educators I endorse your son spending time with are teachers and coaches. Teachers understand their subject matter as well as the different types of learning styles. There should be congruence between pedagogy and learning styles.

Ideally, our boys should be taught by coaches. Coaches understand subject matter and learning styles. But what makes them so effective is that they know you cannot teach a child you have not bonded with, that you do not respect, that you do not understand, and whose culture you do not appreciate.

Magnet Schools

I have a problem with magnet schools. They reinforce classism and elitism. Let's say a city school district has 100 schools, out of which 90 are poor performing and 10 are effective. In order to appease their middle-class population, school districts provide greater resources to the 10 schools. They are given the best teachers, and only certain students are enrolled through selective admission. Some cities only have a 10 percent White population, but their magnet schools have more than 50 percent White students.

There are few African American males in magnet schools. Superintendents and school boards: in the spirit of affirmative action, the percentage of African American boys in your city should equal the percentage of African American boys in magnet schools.

Sometimes you can get your child into one of these schools if you know someone in the school, if you have a connection. Otherwise, your son will have to take a test. God forbid he misses the cut-off score by one point; he will not get in. Parents who know the importance of test taking will enroll their children in test taking courses. America is a test taking country. If you want your son to be admitted into a magnet school, go to college, graduate, become a lawyer, doctor, accountant, or teacher, he must know how to take and pass tests. Listed below are my test taking techniques:

Test-Taking Techniques

1) Relax and encourage yourself throughout the exam. Tell yourself that you will earn a great score.
2) Get a good night's sleep before the test.
3) Stay relaxed; if you begin to get nervous, take a few deep breaths slowly to relax yourself and then get back to work.
4) Read the directions slowly and carefully.
5) If you don't understand the directions on the test, if possible, ask the teacher to explain.
6) Skim through the test so that you have a good idea how to pace yourself.
7) Write down important formulas, facts, definitions, and/or keywords in the margin first so you won't worry about forgetting them.
8) A student scored 79 when told it was a test and scored 121 when told it was a game. Think of the test as a game.
9) Finish the exam. Answer all questions, even if you have to guess.
10) Never stop for a long time on a single question. Place a dot next to the question, and return if time permits. Answer the easy questions first.
11) In a multiple choice test, read all answers before deciding. The first answer may have the least probability and the last answer the greatest. If you choose the first answer with out reading all of them, you will not realize that the last answer included the first.

12) Use the process of elimination. If there are five answer choices, probably three of them do not make sense. You have at least a 50 percent probability with the remaining two answers.

13) Before reading the answer choices, ask yourself what question is being asked. Determine your answer first and then look for it among the answer choices. Do not let multiple answers confuse you.

14) When in doubt, go with your first intuition.

15) Avoid careless mistakes. Place your answer in the right box. If time permits, check your work. Use all the time available. You do not score higher because you finished first.

16) Qualifiers like *never, always,* and *every* mean that the statement must be true all of the time. Usually these types of qualifiers lead to a false answer.

17) If any part of the question is false, then the entire statement is false, but just because part of a statement is true doesn't necessarily make the entire statement true.

18) In true and false tests, every part of a true statement must be true. If any one part of the statement is false, the whole statement is false, despite many true phrases.

19) Pay close attention to negatives, qualifiers, absolutes, and long strings of statements.

20) Negatives can be confusing. If the statement contains negatives such as *no, not,* and *cannot,* drop the negative and read what remains. Decide whether that sentence is true or false. If it is true, its opposite, or negative, is usually false.

21) Qualifiers are words that restrict or open up general statements. Words like *sometimes, often, frequently, ordinarily,* and *generally* open up the possibilities of making accurate statements. They make more modest claims, are most likely to reflect reality, and usually indicate true answers.

22) Absolute words restrict possibilities. *No, never, none, always, every, entirely,* and *only* imply the statement must be true 100 percent of the time, which usually indicates an answer of false.

23) Long sentences often include groups of words set off by punctuation. Pay attention to the truth of each of these phrases. If one is false, it usually indicates a false answer.

24) In "All of the above" and "None of the above" choices, if you are certain one of the statements is true, don't choose "None of the above." If one of the statements is false, don't choose "All of the above."

25) In a question with an "All of the above" choice, if you see at least two correct statements, then "All of the above" is probably the answer.

26) Usually the correct answer is the choice with the most information.

27) Look for key words in test directions and questions such as: *choose, describe, explain, compare, identify, similar, except, not,* and *but.*

28) How can you avoid skipping a line on the answer sheet and thus rendering all subsequent answers wrong? Use a sheet of paper to line up your answers.

29) Many questions use the following words: *trace, support, analyze, explain, infer, summarize, evaluate, compare, formulate, contrast, describe,* and *predict.* You must know the meanings of these words.

Tracking

A practice similar to magnet school procedures is tracking. Here, regular schools divide their children based on test scores. You can have a low achieving school with 10 percent of the student body doing well. These students will be placed in the gifted and talented, honors, and advanced placement track. We must do whatever we can to place our boys in those tracks.

Unfortunately, many boys do not want to go to magnet school or be placed in the highest track because the peer group discourages them from doing well academically.

It is a fine line Black males must walk. They must please both their parents by being academically sound and please their peer group by fighting, playing basketball, and rapping well.

Private and Suburban Schools

Two percent of our children are attending private schools. Many parents use suburban schools as private schools. They tell me their primary concern is to keep their sons safe. They have moved to the suburbs to place their child in a school that has less than a 10 percent Black population and few if any African American teachers. In time, parents will be dismayed to discover that the schools have placed their boys in special education or lower track classes.

This same mindset drives parents to send their sons to private schools. Not only do parents want their boys safe but by choosing private school, they believe they are eliminating negative peer pressure.

They did not choose the school based on how strong the principal and teachers were, if the curriculum was Africentric, if there were single gender classrooms, or if the lesson plans were right-brain. They made the decision to send their sons to suburban or private schools solely based on safety and removing their sons from the negative influence of the peer group.

What a terrible dilemma! You have to choose between ineffective inner city schools where your child may be a victim of gang violence and ineffective private or suburban schools where, although your son may be safer, he is at risk of being referred to special education or the lowest track.

One of the things I like about the Leave No Child Behind program, even though it has never been properly funded, is that it forces all schools, especially suburban schools, to disaggregate their scores. While suburban schools may be high performing overall, there's a wide disparity between the performance of White and Black students. Parents need to be cognizant of that. In the past, this information has not been shared with them.

Charter Schools

There is an increasing number of charter schools. Many of them use the themes discussed earlier, Monterrosi, Kipp,

African Centered, and single gender. There are other themes which include military, entrepreneurship, fine arts, science, international, etc. There has been a great response to charger schools.

Parent Involvement

As age increases, parent involvement must also increase. For some reason, some parents think that as their sons become older, less involvement is required. The opposite is true. With all the negative peer pressure, rap music, video games, and television your teenager is exposed to, he may need you more than your 6 year old. Make sure you stay involved K–12 at the same level. It hurts me when I speak at middle and high schools to see how few parents attend the events compared to those attending at Head Start and the primary grades.

Parent involvement is not just about volunteering at school. You're an involved parent when you make sure your son is doing his homework every night and doing it well. This is an issue of contention between parents and sons. Some parents back off because their sons wear them down on the challenge of homework. Make sure your son is doing a minimum of two hours of homework per night. It may come from the school or you can assign it, but there should be a minimum of two hours of homework. When you read the research and biographies of African American men who excelled in academics, one of the common threads of their success was that their parents put academics first. When I was growing up, I pleaded with my teachers, "Please give me homework, because if you don't, my parents will." I knew my parents' homework would be more challenging than theirs.

Do not nag them about homework. Do not compromise, nor should you do the homework for them. If you make sure they get started as soon as they get home, then they won't be up until midnight trying to get it done. When they get home, homework needs to be their first priority.

Parents, you need to visit your son's school. Research shows that teachers are more compassionate and they have higher expectations of students when parents visit the school and even better, sit in the classroom.

At the beginning of each school year, exchange phone numbers with your son's teachers and give them copies of *Countering the Conspiracy to Destroy Black Boys* and *Keeping Black Boys Out of Special Education.* Teachers were never taught in college about Black male learning styles and culture. You'd be helping them to do a better job with your son.

If your son's number-one job is to be a student, then your number-one job for the next 13 years, K–12, is to make sure he is in the best environment for him to fly and reach his full potential. There is a reason why some parents spend large amounts of money on elite preschools. These schools are called "preschool ivy league colleges." You pay now or you pay later. If we don't provide our children with the best environment K–12, we—and they—may pay for the next 40 years of our—and their—lives.

In the next chapter we will look at the three critical grade levels affecting our sons.

CHAPTER 15: THREE CRITICAL GRADE LEVELS

The three critical grade levels for our boys are kindergarten, fourth grade, and ninth grade. Listed below is a chart from my earlier book *Countering the Conspiracy to Destroy Black Boys*. Please notice how well African American boys are doing K-3 and the marked decline after fourth grade.

Beginning Third Grade Percentile	Ending Seventh Grade Percentile	Reading Progress (Years)
98	35	1.3
97	54	2.7
92	24	2.1
91	68	3.1
81	72	3.9
72	72	3.6
66	59	3.9
63	7	0.7
63	4	0.0
57	39	3.2
47	9	2.1
41	11	2.5
29	12	3.0
21	44	5.6
21	29	4.7
21	17	3.8
18	1	1.3
16	39	4.6
7	30	4.5
5	5	3.2

If you want to see God at His best, look at our boys in kindergarten. They sit in front of the class. They're eager and curious. They love learning. They have a glow in their eyes. Their spirits have not been broken.

If you want to see Satan at his best, stay in the same school and go to a ninth grade class. The boys are no longer sitting in the front. They are sitting in the rear. They are no longer asking questions or curious about anything. They are no longer innocent. There's no glow in their eyes. Their spirits have been broken.

Something happens to our boys as they progress through these three critical grades. I believe the most important grade is fourth. Of all the things I've done with pride in life, other than preaching and bringing people to Christ, is to inspire hundreds of African American males to become classroom teachers, specifically fourth grade teachers. I appeal to my Black male readers to consider teaching, if only for one year—preferably fourth grade.

Looking at the above chart, you can't help but wonder how our boys can do so well K–3 and do so poorly from fourth grade on.

How can a boy score at the 98th percentile at the beginning of the third grade but at the 35th percentile at the end of the seventh grade?

What happens to our boys? In third grade a boy wants to be an engineer, but in seventh grade he wants to be a drug dealer.

What happened? What explains the fourth-grade syndrome?

Parents, do your sons enjoy going to school? A warning sign is when your son no longer wants to go to school.

Unfortunately, as our boys grow older, the desire to attend school decreases. As age increases, school esteem decreases.

Why do our boys want to go to school? When boys are in the early grades, they want to go to school because they want to learn. They love learning. That's their primary reason for going to school. Unfortunately, boys in the upper grades desire to go to school mostly to be with friends or play a sport.

Interestingly, during holidays and spring and summer breaks, students are often bored, not because they want to return to school, they just want to be with their friends or to play on the team. Studying English, reading, math, science, and history has nothing to do with it.

Could the reason for our sons' apathy have anything to do with the way some teachers teach? Teachers who have a *training* style tend to ask students the majority of the questions. Teachers who *educate* students encourage them to ask the questions. Unfortunately, in most schools, as the age of students increases, the questions decrease.

Your son's questions are an excellent benchmark for determining his progress. Is he asking fewer questions?

In schools that train students, the answers to questions are usually predetermined. In high achieving schools, teachers ask students open-ended questions because they want to develop critical thinkers.

Parents, give your son a word problem to solve each day. This will help him develop and strengthen his critical thinking skills. Connect the word problem to sports or hip-hop culture.

We must do all we can to encourage our boys' desire to go to school, ask questions, and develop their critical thinking skills.

Another behavior that increases as students get older is cheating. Seldom will you find a kindergarten child cheating. Younger children believe that school is about learning; therefore they should ask questions.

Unfortunately, as many of our students get older, they also get cynical. They find out that school is not about learning. If school was about learning, students would be encouraged to ask open-ended questions. Students find out that school is about getting a grade any way you can secure it, and cheating is one possibility.

Educators can always tell if they've failed as a teacher when their students cheat. They are telling you in no uncertain terms that they no longer have a love for learning. They have decided that school is nothing but grades. Likewise, as children get older, they find out that getting a job is not based on what you know but *who* you know.

In kindergarten and the primary grades, students receive more nurturing. In the upper grades, our boys are no longer cute, so less nurturing is provided. That is unfortunate.

It has also been shown in research that in the primary grades, the expectations are higher than in the upper grades. That is unfortunate.

Primary grades use a whole-brain pedagogy. There are at least five ways to teach: written, oral, pictures, fine arts, and artifacts. From the fourth grade on, students receive ditto sheets and text books. I've been appealing to teachers for years to go all day Monday without text books and all day Friday without ditto sheets. Children learn in different ways.

In the primary grades, the curriculum is skills oriented. From the fourth grade on, it becomes more content oriented and Eurocentric. African American students are learning all about European culture but nothing about their own heritage. In research on the drop out rate, many students who dropped out said school was boring and irrelevant. We could reduce the drop out rate if we made the curriculum more Africentric or at least multicultural.

Many boys have gone K–3, K–6, and even K–8 without ever having been taught by a male teacher, especially an African American male teacher.

One explanation for the fourth-grade syndrome is that as age increases, peer pressure increases. Much more will be said about peer pressure in a later chapter.

As age increases, parent involvement decreases.

As age increases, children become more cognizant of the larger society. It is difficult to stay academically focused in a neighborhood filled with gangs, drugs, HIV, and other social ills. It is difficult to believe you are going to be the next Dr. Ben Carson in a neighborhood full of men who have not reached their full potential.

Departmentalization

In the primary grades, most students have one teacher. That teacher teaches all subjects. From the fourth grade on, there are many teachers teaching different subjects. Some students may have nine teachers with nine subjects, and no one seems to know the boy's name.

Bill Gates and others are advocates of smaller schools. Many students, especially African American males, don't do well in high schools of 2,000 to 5,000 students and nine different teachers per year. Can you imagine, nine teachers per year equals 36 teachers in four years, and your son may not have bonded with any of them.

Our boys do well K–3 (98th percentile) because in the primary grades the curriculum is skills oriented. We teach *how to* read. From the fourth grade on, it's all about *what* you've read.

Also, from the fourth grade on, homework increases. The expectations and requirements for study are greater. It is more difficult securing an A in geometry in tenth grade than securing an A in addition in first grade. A student can earn an A in addition without studying. To get an A in geometry requires doing homework and studying. For many Black boys, these are two habits that have not been mastered.

Some boys try to cover their pain of inadequacy by becoming the class clown. Can you imagine, you're in ninth grade and your reading and math scores are at a fourth-grade level. It's embarrassing. How can you hope to maintain your spirit?

There is a difference between school-esteem and self-esteem. Educators ask me to help improve their boys' self-esteem. But when I observe the boys on the playground, the basketball court, freestyling and battling (rap), and hanging with their girlfriends, they demonstrate a high level of self-esteem. Educators often do not understand that there is a difference between school-esteem and self-esteem. What they call low self-esteem due to poor academic performance is really low school-esteem.

Educators must be careful when dealing with the male ego. You do not ask a male student (or any student) go up to the board and diagram a sentence or solve a math problem if you aren't sure that the boy is going to be successful. Many boys avoid this terrible experience by becoming the class clown.

The ultimate objective of being the class clown is to be put out of the room. They love it when teachers remove them from class. This alleviates the anguish, embarrassment, and pain that comes from being in an academic setting they are not prepared for. Parents are often unaware that their sons have become class clowns.

How could a parent agree to social promotions? Many schools will pass your son to the next grade not because he is academically proficient but for social reasons. They don't want a 12 year old in a class with 8 year olds.

How could you accept your son being in ninth grade with a fifth-grade reading level?

Are you just noticing that your son is three or four years behind?

I respect parents who decide that their 5-year-old child is not yet ready for kindergarten and that they need to delay enrollment until age 6. Or that a 9-year-old child needs to remain in fourth grade because he's not ready for fifth-grade work.

Some believe the child's self-esteem will be destroyed if he is held back. I believe that greater damage will be done to the child's self-esteem if he is passed to a grade that he cannot handle.

When a student is retained, that means the school failed him. If you keep doing what you've been doing and expect a different outcome, that borders on insanity. It makes no sense to send a student back to the same incompetent teacher, the same irrelevant Eurocentric curriculum, and the same left-brain lesson plan.

If you are going to retain the student, then give him a master teacher, a right-brain lesson plan, an Africentric curriculum, and put him in a single gender classroom.

Parents, do not allow your son to slip. This marked decline from third grade to seventh grade does not happen overnight. If parents check the homework, there should be no surprises on report card pickup day. If you've been checking the homework, you know what his grades are.

Parents must know exactly where their sons stand in reading and math every year, and they must do everything they can to keep them, at minimum, on grade level and, ideally, above grade level. If you ever see your son slip below grade level, immediately contact the school and look for ways to improve his performance and test scores. If the school can't provide the resources necessary, go to your church, local organizations, fraternities, whatever it takes to provide your son with the tutoring he needs.

This marked decline from the 98th percentile to the 35th percentile is unacceptable, and, parents, you must be held accountable. You need to do whatever is necessary to make sure this does not continue.

Believe me, there is a relationship between the schoolhouse and the jailhouse. I don't know if you're aware that some governors determine prison growth based on fourthgrade reading scores.[6]

Let me repeat that. Some governors determine prison growth based on fourth-grade reading scores. Can you imagine, a governor would rather spend $28,000 a year to incarcerate your son in a system that has a recidivism rate of 85 percent than provide $500 for a fourth-grade intervention program that could correct your son's reading problem. It is obvious that balancing the budget is not the major agenda for politicians. They are cognizant that Head Start, Title I, and Pell Grants are cost effective. They know prison is not a cost-effective program.

Prisons are designed to employ poor, White, rural males who couldn't find a job anywhere else. I hope you are aware that of the 40 million Americans living below the poverty line, only 16 million are Black and Latino. The other 24 million are White.

We must save our boys. Black boys are not dropping out of school in 12th grade. They are dropping out in 9th grade on their 16th birthday. They've usually been retained one or two years, they were placed in special education, they were socially promoted to 9th grade, and now they're 16 years old and cannot read. Because it is such an embarrassing experience, and they cannot be a class clown indefinitely, they drop out.

131

The million dollar question is, what is a 16-year-old un-skilled, inexperienced male going to do when he drops out?

Our boys know the odds. They know that if they drop out, they can't even go to the military. They can't work at Wal Mart or McDonald's. They can't go pro in the NBA.

They know that if they make this decision, their only have two options: to become a rapper or the first drug dealer never to be caught. Unfortunately, they believe that being a rapper or drug dealer is preferable to the terrible experience they endured. How unfortunate!

Furthermore, at the high school level, the ratio of students to counselors is sometimes 500:1. How can anyone counsel effectively with a ratio like that?

Your son must receive mentoring and counseling, especially in light of a decision to drop out. In the final chapter of this book, we will look at other alternatives available to parents when their sons have reached this fork in the road.

I must commend the great work that boarding schools such as Piney Woods and others are doing, but this is not the first option for our boys. We must look critically at what's going on in the three grades: kindergarten, fourth, and ninth. We need to put greater emphasis on kindergarten and fourth grade because if the problems extend to the ninth grade without any correction, it's almost too late.

Notice I said *almost*. Malcolm Little became Detroit Red who then became Malcolm X and on to El-Hajj Malik el-Shabazz. It is never too late for our boys. The sooner we intervene, the better. Ideally, we should always be involved and maintain our boys' enthusiasm and desire for learning. Then we won't experience this ninth-grade dilemma that is plaguing our community.

In the next chapter we will look at the two critical subjects our boys must master: reading and algebra.

Chapter 16: Reading/Algebra

The most important subject for your son to master is reading. Nationally, 44 million adults of all races have difficulty using reading, writing, and computational skills in everyday life.

The average American only reads books 86 hours per year (less among African Americans), but they watch more than 2,000 hours of television (greater among African Americans). The reading problem in America is not just an African American problem. It is a national problem.

In 1955, Rudolf Flesch wrote the groundbreaking book, *Why Johnny Can't Read*. Thirty years later he wrote the sequel, *Why Johnny Still Can't Read*. There have been other significant books, including Jonathan Kozol's *Illiterate America*.

There is a crisis in America in the area of reading, and it is exacerbated in Black America and acute among Black males. Remember, some governors determine prison growth based on fourth-grade reading scores. They believe that poor reading ability is a precursor for crime. It is an indicator of whether or not a person is going to do well in America.

In my book *Keeping Black Boys Out of Special Education* I document that 83 percent of the students placed in special education are not there because of attention deficit disorder (ADD). They are there because they have a reading deficiency.

If the crisis is in reading, then the individualized educational plan (IEP) should document what the school will do differently in reading instruction. If the boy is being placed in special education because of a reading deficiency, then the educational plan should look at whether whole-brain reading or the sight approach to reading is best in each individual case. I believe phonics should be considered. Definitely an Africentric curriculum should be included in the plan. Phonics and an African-centered curriculum are the two best ways to improve reading skills for African American boys.

Some people have difficulty pronouncing my name, Jawanza Kunjufu. This could not be solved with a word approach to reading. The word approach depends upon the word being used frequently within the context of a sentence so the child begins to recognize it. The sight approach to reading involves connecting words to pictures.

Unfortunately, in the late 1950s, America moved away from phonics. Phonics is labor intensive. Publishers of text books make more money with the word and sight approaches to reading than with phonics. If a child knows phonics, there is literally no word he or she cannot pronounce. So it becomes easy to pronounce my name, Jawanza Kunjufu, if you know phonics. If your son needs additional reading instruction, I strongly recommend a phonics-based curriculum.

The content of the curriculum must be relevant. In remedial programs, especially in the middle school and high school grades, the challenge is to provide reading materials that have high content but require low vocabulary skills. If you're serving African American children, the content needs to be either African centered or hip-hop centered. My book *Hip-Hop Street Curriculum* is used successfully by many schools because our children highly value hip-hop culture.

If 83 percent of special education students are there because of a reading deficiency, we should help them maintain grade level by teaching them to read.

Almost 1.5 million African American males are either on probation, in jail, or in state or federal institutions. Unfortunately, 90 percent of them entered jail illiterate. If we simply taught our boys how to read, we'd have a 90 percent chance of keeping them out of jail. Can you imagine how embarrassing it is to ask the security guard to read your girlfriend's letter because you can't?

Ironically, although 90 percent of inmates entered jail illiterate, once in prison they read more than free people. Remember, the average American only spends 86 hours reading books per year. Inmates read far more than that. I'm in the book publishing business, and our largest customer base is prisoners. How unfortunate it is that our males have to go to jail before they learn and love to read. The potential was within them all along. The desire was also there, but it took prison to provide the opportunity to learn.

Parents, let's not rely on prisons to turn our young men into readers. That's something we can do at home.

Children are actors, and they act out what they see in us. When was the last time they saw you read? Is there a reading hour in your home? It would be great if for one hour each night you turned off the television and the entire family read together.

A family that reads together stays together.

Gender Differences

Boys and girls really are different. They mature at different rates. There's almost a three year difference in the maturation rate of boys and girls K–12.

Girls also have stronger verbal skills. Females have 20 percent more nerve tissue connecting the left and right hemispheres of the brain.

At a workshop I conducted in Minnesota, a White female teacher stood up and shared with the audience that she had decided to homeschool her two sons. Now remember, she's a public school teacher, but she chose homeschooling because she refused to allow the school system to force her sons to read before they were ready. She didn't want her sons in special education just because they were not reading at the arbitrary age set by the system.

Research shows that many girls have a desire to read between kindergarten and second grade. For boys, this desire occurs between second and fifth grades. That's what happened to this teacher's sons. One of the sons did not gravitate to reading until fourth grade, and then all he wanted to read were car magazines. The other son started in third grade. Once they started reading, she put them back in public school. They are now at the 90th percentile in reading. This mother realized she needed to take charge of her sons' growth and development. Let this be a lesson for all parents reading this book.

If boys don't read when public schools say they should read, they are labeled ADD (attention deficit disorder) and placed in special education. You cannot allow the public school system to dictate to you when your son should read. Some allowances should be made for maturation differences.

When your son is ready to read, he will tell you. Provide him with material he wants to read. Who would want to read a boring book?

In many households, there are more CDs and DVDs than books. Unfortunately today, our boys are watching television and playing video games far more than they are reading. Televisions are almost in every room. It's as if we cannot do without television. For many of us, television is a drug. If you don't believe it, try turning it off for an hour or a day and see how well you function. If we're going to raise our boys to become successful, we need to turn off the TV and have them open a book.

On a daily basis, how many hours does your son watch television? How many minutes does he read? The answers to these questions will let you know how to fix any reading problems he may have.

Governors do not determine prison growth based on the number of hours that your child watches television. They determine prison growth based on your son's reading deficiency.

Habits are significant. It has been said that if you do something for 14 consecutive days, you will do it for the rest of your life. If we had parents who, with their preschool boys, had reading hour every night, I believe the kids would love to read for the rest of their lives. If children were raised to believe that the last hour before bed was for reading a story or the Bible, not watching HBO, BET, or Showtime, we could turn this tide around.

Because reading is so fundamental, your son's reading level is a critical benchmark. It is difficult to do anything in America as an illiterate person. Many of our boys act like class clowns because they know they are illiterate and they cannot keep up with the class pace. We must do everything possible to strengthen our sons' reading skills.

Algebra

Algebra is the gatekeeping subject to college. It is the language of computers and a subject that emphasizes critical thinking skills. Unfortunately, many of our boys don't fully understand the importance of this subject because they dropped out in ninth grade before they had their first algebra class.

In America, 1 percent of the population owns 48 percent of the wealth. Ten percent of the population owns 86 percent of the wealth. The children of the wealthy take their first algebra class not in ninth or tenth grade but in fourth or fifth grade. The latest they take algebra is in eighth grade. The children of the poor take algebra between ninth and tenth grades.

Expose your son to algebra as early as possible. When my wife and I were raising our boys, we gave them a word problem every night for desert. One of the reasons why we did this was because many children know how to add, subtract, multiply, and divide but they do not know when to use those operations in a word problem. If you want to train a child, supply the skill first. If you want to educate a child, supply the need f What good is it to add, subtract, multiply, and divide and not know when to use those operations? That's why in America you can have a BA, MA, and PhD and still be unemployed. You might know how to manage someone else's business, but you do not know how to start your own.

Our children know how to solve problems, but they do not know how to set them up. To solve a word problem, you have to set it up. The beauty of algebra is that it requires critical thinking skills. You are solving for the unknown. There is no reason why algebra has to be delayed until eighth, ninth, or tenth grade. Algebra can be taught to kindergarten students— and they are not afraid of the unknown. Research has clearly documented that the best time to teach a foreign language is when children are in preschool and the primary grades. The same applies to algebra.

Because young children are so curious, they enjoy exploring the unknown. We need to encourage our boys to become more math oriented. Teachers and administrators love to tell me that our boys are not into math. Yet, you'll find these same boys, without pencil, paper, or calculator, converting kilos to grams and grams to dollar bills. These boys know math when it's drug math. They know math when it's related to hip-hop record sales or the NBA. Teachers may be pleasantly surprised at the effectiveness of using NBA math when students have to figure out a player's three-point shooting percentage, free throw shooting percentage, and his assist-to-rebound ratio. The same thing applies to the NFL: rushing yards, passing yards, receiving yards.

We need to make math real. The problem in algebra is that many teachers are left-brain oriented, and they're trying to teach math to right-brain learners.

I strongly encourage everyone to read *How to Teach Math to Black Students* by Shahid Muhammad and *The Algebra Project* by Robert Moses. These authors advocate moving math from the abstract to the concrete. In preschool and primary programs, we recommend using the abacus. Likewise, dominos can be seen and held in the hands.

Robert Moses recommends that we connect the integer line to the students' city area (north side, south side, east side, west side). Remember, integers are whole numbers, negative whole numbers, and zero. So the integer line looks like this, with more or fewer numbers as needed:

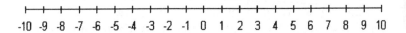

The integer line can also be connected to climate—above and below zero temperatures. The point here is that children need to visualize the integer line.

Shahid Muhammad recommends connecting geometry to pizzas and pies. Again, the point is that children need to be able to see and touch the math. Our boys are brilliant in math if we teach them from a right-brain perspective.

Algebra is an important subject on the SAT and ACT; unfortunately, our students are not properly prepared for those tests. They're so far behind when they enter ninth grade that their first class in math is basic math, business math, or general math; then maybe they'll get algebra in their junior or senior year. When they take the SAT and ACT, it's possible they have never had an algebra class for even one year. They have not taken algebra II, geometry, trigonometry, or calculus, and that's why their scores are so low.

Charles Murray, it has nothing to do with genetics. It's all about exposure. To look at how well children are doing academically, simply investigate the information they have been exposed to. The problem is that Black boys are not being exposed to algebra until it's too late. They're dropping out in ninth grade before they experience their first algebra class.

How many mathematicians have we lost in the African American male community because we waited so late to expose them to algebra?

It is a national embarrassment that 86 percent of the NBA is African American but only 2 percent of the engineers and doctors. How many Black boys could be engineers and doctors but because of the failure of the public school system will never tap into that potential?

Words are more powerful than bombs. Parents, never say you were not good in math or science because you are then promoting a genetic argument. If that's what you feel, please keep it to yourself. We cannot afford to negatively influence our boys at this critical juncture.

Parents who want to move from the inner city to the suburbs are naive and clueless to the fact that while the school looks integrated on the outside, it may be highly segregated on the inside. Never forget that our Black children may receive only general and basic math while other children are taking courses in algebra I and II, geometry, trigonometry, and calculus.

Our students are being counseled to take only two to three years of math. Parents, you must do everything possible to ensure that your son stays in school beyond ninth grade and that he takes four years of math and science. Our boys think they are getting by when they don't have to take algebra II to graduate. But when they go to college, they have to take remedial math because they are ineligible to take college algebra. At this pace, it will take them seven years to graduate.

Galatians 6:7 says, "God will not be mocked. You reap what you sow." If our boys are not required to take a rigorous academic class load, they will pay dearly when they go to college.

Parents, insist that your sons take algebra as soon as possible. The sooner our boys are exposed to algebra, the more successful they will become.

In the next chapter, we will look at America's new form of segregation, and that's special education.

Chapter 17: Special Education

Is there a relationship between special education and prison?

Is there a relationship between illiteracy and incarceration?

Is there a relationship between Ritalin and cocaine?

Is special education the new form of segregation?

Why do White girls have the least chance of being placed in special education and Black boys the greatest?

Is it possible that a parent would agree to place her child in special education to receive a $400 SSI check? Would a parent really sell her child for $400 a month?

Why do they call it *special* education?

After being in special education for several years, do Black boys return to the mainstream classroom at grade level?

What does special education do to the self-esteem of Black boys?

Does your son believe he can pass without studying?

Does your son believe he is invincible? (That is why God gave him parents.)

Quality time is not going to a ballgame, movie, or amusement park with your son. Quality time is when you sit on his bed with no agenda and listen to him.

Without a high school diploma, Black males are obsolete.

Does special education destroy our boys' spirit?

There is a thin line between ADD (attention deficit disorder) and Black boys being placed in gifted and talented classes.

Only 27 percent of special education students graduate from high school.

Only 10 percent return to and remain in the mainstream classroom.

A Black boy was given math problems to solve in 45 minutes. Because he was a brilliant student, he did the problems in less than 30 minutes. His teacher, who had low expectations and poor classroom management skills, did not give him any additional work for the last 15 minutes. So he decided to talk and play with his classmates. He was politely removed from the class and written up and labeled ADD. The reality was that the boy was at the 90th percentile in mathematics, was not being challenged by his teacher, and should have been placed in an honors math class. The problem was not with the boy. It was the teacher, his parents, and the school system. The school system should have placed him in a gifted and talented class. At the very least, he should have been given a better teacher. Unfortunately, the boys' parents did not have the skills or interest to advocate for and protect their son. As a result, we lost another boy.

Another boy was taken out of the regular fourth grade class because he was a year or two behind in reading. He was placed in special education, but the IEP did not correctly diagnose and correct his reading deficiency. As a result, he was in special education for several years and is now being returned to the mainstream classroom in eighth grade, further behind.

Let's try and understand the special education experience from the Black boy's perspective. It is traumatic to be taken out of a mainstream classroom to begin with. He is labeled retarded by his peer group, so he has to find ways to protect what little self-esteem he has left. He definitely does not have self-esteem in the academic arena. He accentuates his self-esteem in the areas of fighting, rapping, and sports. When he is mainstreamed back into a regular classroom, he is even further behind. This exacerbates the experience, and he becomes even more embarrassed. If he could drop out in eighth grade he would, but he's only 14 or 15. He will wait until ninth grade when he is 16 years old to drop out.

All of this could have been avoided. Remember those teachers I call referral agents? The referral agent is the culprit in this scenario. Research shows that 20 percent of the teachers make 80 percent of the referrals to special education. When a teacher refers a child to special education, there's a 92 percent chance he will be tested and a 73 percent he will be placed in special education. Although schools tend to side with the teacher, a strong administrator will not accept a disproportionate number of Black boys being placed in special education because of referral agents.

High achieving schools have an academic team or a pre-referral team. Any teacher who recommends that a child be placed in special education goes before this intervention team first. In *Keeping Black Boys Out of Special Education* I offer 86 mainstreaming strategies that the classroom teacher can use before referring a child to special education. Research indicates that pre-referral intervention teams have reduced special education placements in schools by more than 90 percent.

Gender learning and behavioral differences account for the disproportionate placement of Black boys in special education. Many teachers have not taken classes in male learning styles and male culture. If we know that boys have a shorter attention span, teachers should shorten the lesson or break it up and spread it out throughout the day or a couple of days. Boys have a high energy level, so teachers should allow more movement.

Did you know there are schools being built without playgrounds?

Did you know there are schools that no longer offer recess?

Did you know there are schools that have cut physical education, despite the fact that boys have a high energy level and too many are overweight and obese? We could reduce special education placements if we offered P.E. on a daily basis and allowed more movement in the classroom.

We know that girls are more advanced in fine motor skills and boys, gross motor. Should we provide more objects, more artifacts, in the classroom?

Girls can hear three times better than boys, so who should sit in the front of the class?

These are only a few of the gender differences that impact learning. We have developed female-oriented classrooms for male students. There's nothing wrong with our boys. There's something wrong with our classrooms.

On the other hand, parents need to meet schools halfway. They need to do everything possible to improve their sons' attention span. The following will help:

1. Reduce television viewing.
2. Increase reading.
3. Have them play games that improve concentration.
4. Reduce, if not eliminate, sugar consumption.
5. Reduce, if not eliminate, all processed foods that are filled with additives.

Parents, make sure your child receives a thorough medical exam that assesses ears, eyes, blood, thyroid gland, dental, and nutritional deficiencies. Many of our boys could have avoided special education if they had simply been given a pair of eyeglasses. Some boys have allergies that have not been detected.

One of the most important meetings of your son's life is the IEP (Individual Educational Plan). It is a highly intimidating meeting. Attendees include the principal, classroom teacher, social worker, psychologist, special education coordinator, and parent. The following will help you take charge of the entire process on behalf of your son.

1. Mothers, do not attend the IEP meeting alone. Studies have found that when mothers attend the meeting with another male, ideally a male professional (psychologist, social worker, or educator), the outcome is improved.
2. If possible, document how well your son did in the previous year with a different teacher. The problem is not always with our boys but with custodians, referral agents, and instructors.
3. Request that before even considering special education your son be given a different teacher, preferably a master teacher in that particular grade. If that's not possible, you may want to consider moving your son out of that school. Remember, two consecutive years of an ineffective teacher could destroy your son's life.
4. Before the referral is even considered, the 86 mainstream strategies from my book *Keeping Black Boys Out of Special Education* should be implemented by

the classroom teacher. Everyone on that committee should receive a copy of my book. Parents need to know their rights. The committee may not tell you that your child cannot be tested or given drugs without your permission. Once you agree, they have almost *carte blanche* privileges to do whatever they want.

5. The child cannot be placed in special education without first being tested. Do not be intimidated into believing that your son has to take the test given to him. All tests are not created equally. Avoid the Wechsler and Stanford Binet tests. Tell the team that the only tests that you will consider are the Black Intelligence Test, the System of Multicultural Pluralistic Assessment, the Learning Potential Assessment Device, or the Kaufman Assessment. Under no circumstances should you accept the Wechsler or the Stanford Binet.

6, If the test determines that your son does need special education, be sure the IEP is very clear. There's an 83 percent chance that what your son needs is improvement in reading. Don't let them talk you into giving your son Ritalin. There is no research to show that Ritalin improves reading scores. Phonics and a culturally relevant curriculum improve reading scores, not Ritalin. Do not sign off on the IEP if it does not clearly document how the school is going to improve your son's reading.

7. The components that you should look for in the reading program are a smaller student-teacher ratio, a master teacher, a phonics-based, and Africentric or multicultural curriculum. If the IEP does not include all of the above, then please do not sign. If the deficiency is primarily in reading, then special education should be viewed as a resource, not the final destination. Ideally, the reading teacher should come into your son's mainstream classroom. It would be much better for your son to remain in the mainstream classroom and have the special education resources brought to him.

The other option is that your son only leaves the mainstream classroom for a limited amount of time, primarily for reading instruction. The rest of the day your son should remain in the regular classroom. Do everything possible to avoid having your child placed in a contained special education classroom for the entire school day.

8. Progress should be monitored on a monthly basis. If the problem is reading, monitor reading progress on a monthly basis. At some point, your child should be brought up to speed and no longer need special education resources. You must work with the school. While the school is providing additional instruction for your son, you need to do your part. No child in special education should be watching television Sunday through Thursday night. We need to revisit our priorities at home. There should be very little time to play outside during the school week. All recreational activities (listening to music, playing video games, playing with friends) should be greatly reduced until the problem is resolved. Only 27 percent of special education students graduate from high school. You cannot simply sit back and allow your son to be placed in special education and then expect some tremendous improvement without your involvement. The research does not bear out that experience.

9. If your son has been referred to special education and he is in fifth, sixth, seventh, or eighth grade, this is a crisis, and you should treat it as such. There's no better time to homeschool your son or transfer him to one of the schools I recommended earlier (Christian, single gender, Montessori, African centered, KIPP Academy). Something needs to be done because the answer is not special education.

In the next chapter, we will look at the number one influence on our children, and that's peer pressure.

Chapter 18: Peer Pressure

Can you imagine that the greatest influence on your son is not you?

Did you know that your son's peer group will determine his grade point average? In fact, the peer group may determine whether he graduates.

The peer group may determine whether your son goes to college.

The peer group may determine the major he declares (if he goes to college).

The peer group may determine whether he earns $8 an hour or $80 an hour.

The peer group may determine whether he lives to be 90 years old or dies before his 21st birthday.

The peer group may determine whether he becomes a drug dealer, rapper, ball player, engineer, doctor, or lawyer.

Peer pressure is the number one influence on your son.

In the next three chapters, we will look at the three main influences on your son: peer pressure, rap music, and television/video games. First, we will tackle the greatest influence of all, and that's peer pressure.

- In 1950, the greatest influences were home, school, and church.
- In 2007, the greatest influences are peer pressure, rap, and television.

I believe the selection of your friends is the third most important decision in your life, after God and marriage. Unfortunately, peer pressure can affect those decisions.

It's frightening to realize that your son's peer group may have a greater influence on his life than you do. Parents, please read this chapter very carefully.

Do your son's friends know him better than you?

Do you really know your son?

Do you know what he likes and dislikes?

What are the three most important issues in your son's life?

Children have become very astute. They know what to say to their parents, and they know what to say to their friends. Is there a difference between what your son talks about with you and what he talks about with his friends? What is he really all about?

When fathers only spend 7 minutes and mothers 34 minutes with their boys, peer pressure becomes all consuming. If we're going to usurp the authority of peer pressure, we're going to have to increase the time we spend with our children. That may mean having dinner or watching television together as a family. It may require reading together as a family. Praying, studying the Bible, and going to church together would definitely increase the time and quality of communication with your son.

Some children do not see their parents for the entire week. The peer group is actually raising our boys.

There is an inverse relationship between peer pressure and self-esteem. If you have strong self-esteem, you are less influenced by peer pressure. If you have low self-esteem, you are highly influenced by peer pressure.

I believe that peer pressure is greater on males than females. Unfortunately, the male peer group has defined what it means to be a man. This is not in the best interest of our boys.

There is a pecking order in male peer groups. When it's time to play basketball and there are ten players and each team will choose five, the pecking order will determine who will be picked first. After a while, you begin to know where you are in the pecking order. It is a challenge to your self-esteem to be picked last.

There is a pecking order among males and females. If you're in an eighth-grade class where there are 15 boys and 15 girls, the pecking order determines the most popular children. Females who are considered beautiful are first in the pecking order. Males who are considered handsome are first in the order. Males who are considered cool, who can fight, who dress nicely, can rap, who are tall—they are first. It is a tremendous challenge and threat to a male's self-esteem if he cannot play basketball, if he's not considered handsome, if he doesn't have the latest gym shoes and clothes, and is short.

Adults are not usually aware of what our boys feel is the most important factor in their lives, and that's where the peer group places them in the pecking order.

Peer groups are so powerful they literally can place our boys in a box. This is what Blacks do, and this is what Whites do. The Black male peer group has determined that the number one sport is basketball, and football is second. All other sports fall completely off the radar.

It is troubling that at integrated schools, the starting five on the basketball team are all Black, and the science fair participants, spelling bee team members, math team, and debate team are all White. The Black peer group has determined that this is what we do. Anyone who breaks rank is ostracized.

For a Black male to be involved in the science fair, debate team, spelling bee team, and any other academic club is suicide if he cannot fight, play basketball, rap, and dress nicely. It is different for girls. It is acceptable for girls to be on the honor roll and in AP classes and still be accepted by their peer group.

The female peer group also ostracizes Black males who are interested in academics. Ironically, adult women are looking for academically strong Black men, but as girls, they discourage elementary, high school, and even college males who want to pursue academics.

Black males make up 86 percent of the NBA but only 2 percent of the engineers and doctors in this country. What impact has the Black male peer group had on this phenomenon? Why is there such a difference between the nerd and the jock in the way they are treated?

In the Black college movie *Drumline*, Jason Weaver's character has to sneak around just to joyfully study his academic passion: mathematics. Because of his strange behavior throughout the movie, we are led to believe that he may be involved in drugs or worse. It is a real surprise to discover that his "subversive" activity is studying math. Unfortunately, art imitated life in this movie. It is a sad commentary on the Black male peer group that males must hide their love of learning from their friends. How many of our boys feel they must go underground to learn and study their favorite subjects? There's something wrong here.

Many boys try to walk the fine line in trying to be smart for their parents and cool for their friends. Seldom do they ask themselves, "What do I want to do? Do I really want to be an engineer? Do I really like science? Would I like to spend time at the museum?"

Trying to please two masters, like the Bible says, is impossible. You'll become schizophrenic. When boys attempt to satisfy and appease their parents and at the same time comply with their peer group, this can make them insane. Why? Because parents and the peer group are operating from two completely different sets of standards, values, ethics, and norms, all of which are usually in perpetual conflict.

There are parents who have sacrificed and done everything they could to place their sons in the most academically stimulating environment. They spent $20,000 a year to send their son to a private school. They moved to an affluent suburb with high property taxes because they wanted the best for their son. The parents were not even aware that their son, who was recommended for AP or honors classes, refused the challenge because he wanted to be down with his peer group.

Parents, share the following statements with your sons:

- **Show me your friends, and I will show you your future.**
- **The group you run with will be the group you end up with.**
- **If you want to be an engineer, run with the honor roll students. If you want to be a drug dealer, run with the students cutting class.**
- **There is a difference between a friend and an associate. A friend will never backstab you. A friend will never lie about you. A friend will never set you up. Most importantly, a friend will never make you feel like a fool for wanting to do well in school. Be honest, how many friends do you really have?**

Boys walk the fine line between what their parents value and what their friends value by getting good grades but hiding their intelligence from their friends. They don't study. They don't take books home. This behavior can work in the early grades, but from the upper grades on, it is difficult to carry an A without studying.

Some males have found that it is okay to be on the honor roll if they can fight and play basketball. The challenge here is that at some point, your son is going to have to leave the basketball court and go home and study. This is a major test in peer pressure.

Does your son have the strength to leave the basketball court to go home and study for a test?

Fighting is a major issue for our boys. Boys say they could walk away from a fight if it's just two of them, but with the peer group circling, it is difficult to walk away. They cannot withstand the pressure. They would drop down in the pecking order if they walked away. Clearly, the peer group could care less about your son. All they want to see is blood, and not their own.

Parents, role play these scenarios with your son so he can know how to respond to various situations. More will be said about this in the chapter on safety, gangs, and drugs.

I hate to tell you this, mothers, but your son will have to know how to defend himself because he will find himself in a fight, probably several, during his boyhood. The male peer group requires its members to know how to fight. Your son will never gain the peer group's respect if he cannot fight. All this goes on without parents having any idea of what our boys have to deal with every day.

The peer group determines whether your son smokes or drinks. Can you imagine, whether your son has lung cancer, cirrhosis of the liver, or loses 20 to 30 years of his life will depend on his selection of peers. Here is another destiny to be determined by the peer group:

Drug Abuse Deaths (per year)

Heroin	8,000
Cocaine	15,000
Alcohol	100,000
Cigarettes	434,000

People are not dying as much from hard drugs as they are from the softer drugs. Satan doesn't start you on the hard stuff first. He starts you on beer and cigarettes, and then he'll move you to the next level.

Parents, are you absolutely sure how your son would handle the pressure to drink and smoke? Your son is at a party. All of a sudden, cigarettes and reefer are passed around the room. What will be your son's response?

Your son is at a party, and the beer and wine get passed around the room. What will be your son's response?

Alcohol use by persons under 21 is a major public health problem. Alcohol is the most commonly used and abused drug among youth in the United States, more than tobacco and illicit drugs. Although drinking by persons under 21 is illegal, people age 12 to 20 years drink almost 20 percent of all alcohol consumed in the United States.

Parents, if you are waiting until your son's 16th birthday to discuss drinking, smoking, and sex education, you are four to eight years too late. Young people drink and smoke because of peer pressure. Most youth smoke their first cigarette by the time they are 13 years old.

What should we do to usurp the authority of the peer group?

The most important role models for young people are their parents. Being a parent is a 24/7 responsibility. One of the best ways to encourage your son to be a scholar and a leader is for you to be the same. It is difficult to persuade your son not to drink or smoke if he sees you doing it. Boys don't respect "Do as I say, not as I do."

Parents tell me they value academics, but their son doesn't. They don't smoke, but their son does. They don't drink, but their son does. In spite of being the best role model you can be, this is not a foolproof way to protect your son or to ensure that he does well academically.

What else can parents do?

We can physically show the impact that smoking has on the brain and lungs using pictures. The media loves portraying people looking the picture of health as they smoke and drink. Satan loves to show us the picture on the front end. He doesn't want you to see the consequences of such behaviors. We need to show our boys how people look after years of smoking and drinking. They need to see how a liver looks that has been abused by alcohol.

Athletics can be used to discourage young people from drinking and smoking. I like track because it is difficult, if not impossible, to be a runner and a smoker. Unfortunately, some athletes claim they can smoke and drink during their off seasons. Some have even told me they play better when they are high. I don't believe that, but they do believe it.

Athletes who are involved in many different sports throughout the year have less time to indulge in drugs. Hopefully, we can impress upon our students that to reach their full potential, they need to avoid alcohol, drugs, and cigarettes.

Young people really do believe they drink because they want to drink and smoke because they want to smoke. They don't realize they have been fully persuaded by advertising and marketing campaigns. In 2007, a 30-second commercial during the Superbowl cost almost $3 million. Why would a company spend $3 million for only 30 seconds if they were not absolutely sure our children would be convinced to drink what they want them to drink and buy the shoes they want them to buy. Advertisers see youth between the ages of 12 and 18 as their best, most profitable market.

Parents, discuss peer pressure, smoking, drinking, and drugs early with your son. The lines of communication must be always kept open. We cannot belatedly walk into our 16-year-old son's bedroom and expect to have the first meaningful discussion about the pecking order, how peer pressure affects him academically and socially, and how his peers influence his smoking, drinking, and sexual involvement.

I like to use visual images with young people to reinforce my points. We need to meet youth where they are. So watch television shows and even negative rap videos with your son.

Listen to his music with him. Play video games with him. Use these moments to teach. Unfortunately, our youth are watching television with their peer group, which is like the blind leading the blind. They are not receiving the direction they need from their parents.

There is a powerful scene in *Boyz n the Hood* where Cuba Gooding is with his friends in a car. There is a distinction between peer pressure and self-esteem. Cuba Gooding is on his way to Morehouse. He is the only one in the car with something to lose. He'd had numerous conversations with his father. His father not only talked to him, he listened to him. They had dialogue. Cuba Gooding has enough strength internally to know that although he doesn't want to be ostracized from the peer group, he has to walk away. The beauty of that scene is that the peer group respects Cuba's decision.

When I was a track runner in high school, the gangs left me alone. In fact, they told me to run faster because I was making them proud to be in the neighborhood. I did run faster because of what the gangs said to me.

When gangs see there's something in you, that you are about something, they respect that. They see the strength within you. We need to help our sons reach that level of self-esteem where they not only feel good about themselves but the peer group feels proud of them as well.

Invite your son's friends over to the house like Mary Thomas did. There are certain homes where the peer group likes to congregate, and hers was one. Now, if you are trying to be buddy buddy with your son, that's a problem. Some parents drink, smoke, and watch porno videos with their children. They let them have sex and do drugs in the home, believing it is safer under their roof than out in the street. That's not what I'm talking about.

I'm talking about conscientious parents who are ready to fight fire with fire. Since the peer group is so influential, these parents invite the group into their home so they can have more influence, control, and make a difference.

Invite your son's friends over so you can get to know them better. Show me your son's friends, and I'll show you his future. This is the Law of Association. Parents must do everything possible to know their children's friends as well as they know their child.

Also, invite the parents of your son's friends over for a visit. Discuss all the issues together so that you will be on the same page and will speak with one voice.

Richard Majors wrote a powerful book titled *Cool Pose: The Dilemmas of Black Manhood in America.* He asserts that there's something almost magical to our boys about hanging out on the corner together. They know they're not doing well in school. They know that the females are outperforming them. It's not that they're not cognizant of that. Being with their friends with their shoes untied, pants going the wrong way, underwear showing, listening to rap, and talking about sports is the greatest thrill of all. This trance-like behavior is so enticing that many lack the strength to leave that corner culture to go home and study.

How much time does your son spend on the street?

How much time does your son spend on the corner?

How much idle time does your son have?

Parents, you must address these issues if you are serious about having an academically successful son.

Too many of our boys have too much idle time. Too much time hanging on corners. Too much time on the street. We need to reprogram that time with positive activities, and we will look at some in the chapter on the "village."

In the next chapter, we will examine the second greatest influence on our sons, and that is rap music.

Chapter 19: Rap Music

Gangsta rap is not Black culture. It's BMG, EMI, Time Warner, and Universal culture.

Gangsta rappers want to get paid.

The real issue is not Don Imus. Gangsta rappers, BMG, EMI, Time Warner, and Universal are the issue.

Eighty percent of gangsta rap is bought by White youth. They buy few conscious, positive, Africentric, or gospel rap CDs. Why?

Are gangsta rappers the new minstrel show, reinforcing White stereotypes?

Are the rappers raising your son?

Rap is the number-two influence on our youth. Notice I didn't say hip-hop. There's a distinction between rap and hip-hop. hip-hop is much larger than rap music. hip-hop represents the culture, a culture of change and young people. hip-hop encompasses not only music but hair styles, fashions, language—the entire lifestyle.

Parents, young people will not respect us if we do not make a distinction between hip-hop and rap music. Within the context of hip-hop is rap music. Even within the context of rap music, not all rap is gangsta rap. We must take care not to lump all rap tunes into one genre. There are numerous types of rap music, but I won't get into East Coast, West Coast, the South, Jamaican, etc. Instead, I will frame this discussion with three broad categories of rap music:

1. Conscious/positive rap. Some of the popular artists in conscious/positive rap are Talib, Common, and Kanye.
2. Gospel rap. I recommend the various artists on the CD "Holy hip-hop" (volumes 1–4).
3. Gangsta rap. This category includes people like Snoop, The Game, and 50 Cent.

Young people will try to convince you they are only into the beat, but they underestimate their brain, which is a computer that downloads both the beat and the lyrics.

During slavery, control was around the wrist and the ankles. In the new form of slavery, the chains are around the mind. Primarily, it is perpetuated in the music.

There are four powerful companies that control the distribution of the music: EMI, Universal, Time Warner, and BMG (which acquired Sony).

EMI	27 Wrights Lane
Universal	2440 Sepulveda Blvd. Suite 100 Los Angeles, CA 90064
Time Warner	75 Acapella Plaza New York, NY 10019
BMG	550 Madison Ave. New York, NY 10022

Connect the dots on what's happening in the genre of gangsta rap. I like rap music. My concern is the overemphasis on gangsta rap.

These four companies have more than 5,000 songs to choose from, yet the same 40 songs are played over and over again on the radio. They use the N word, the B word, the H word, the MF word, and whatever other vile word they can use to perpetuate a negative stereotype.

Gangsta rap is not Black culture. Gangsta rap is corporate culture. Gangsta rap is EMI, Universal, Time Warner, and BMG. We must do everything we can to protect our boys from the onslaught of gangsta rap.

The following resources are presented here because they go into far more detail than I can in one chapter on this very important subject.

- My book *Hip-Hop Street Curriculum: Keeping It Real*
- Byron Hurt's documentary *Hip-Hop: Beyond Beats*
- *Hip-Hop Generation* by Bakari Kitwana
- *The gospel Remix: Reaching the Hip-Hop Generation* by Ralph Watkins
- Paula Zahn's CNN documentary *Hip-Hop: Art or Poison?*

Dr. Cohen's study "The Black Youth Project." Dr. Cohen listened to youth and reported their concerns. More than half the youth were not pleased with rap music and the overemphasis on gangsta rap.

We all know about the fallout that came from Don Imus' comments. Many people felt that the punishment was too harsh and that he didn't say anything different from what Black gangsta rappers have said in their music.

Others went after the gangsta rappers. In the Paula Zahn documentary *Hip-Hop: Art or Poison?,* rappers said that if they tried to provide conscious rap like KRS-1, it would be difficult, if not impossible, to secure a contract. The contracts go to the artists who are doing gangsta rap.

The four companies will say they are simply producing what sells. Gangsta rap sells more than any other genre in rap music. They say that if Black women in particular are concerned about not being called the B word and the H word, they should not buy the music.

The reality is that African Americans only buy 20 to 30 percent of gangsta rap. Seventy to 80 percent of gangsta rap tunes are purchased by White youth. The million dollar question is, Why do White youth love gangsta rap?

Is there a relationship between the gangsta rappers and the minstrel shows of the early 1900s?

Do White youth love gangsta rap because the music confirms what they believe about Black people?

Is there a relationship between White youth buying gangsta rap and white college students dressing up at Halloween parties like gangsta rappers (gold grills) and other negative, stereotypical images of Black people?

Racists want to make it appear that gangsta rap and Black culture are synonymous, but gangsta rap is not Black culture.

When Don Imus made his comment about the African American scholar-athletes at Rutgers University, many rushed to compare him with gangsta rappers. Snoop Dogg took issue with the comparison. He said when gangsta rappers use the B and H words in their music, they are not referring to women who are doing something with their lives. He said gangsta rappers are talking about a certain type of female in the hood. Unfortunately, many rappers think it makes sense to call the neighborhood females Hs and Bs—that's okay.

I really respect Spelman for telling Nelly that he could not perform on campus until he apologized and cleaned up the video "Tip Drill," where a credit card is slid through a woman's anus. *Essence* magazine and Spelman have a movement called Take Back the Music. Unfortunately, these women have not received the media coverage Don Imus received.

Mothers, listen to Tupac's song "Mama." It is important that adults do not put all rappers in one category. However, as Gil Scott Heron mentioned, you can't have it both ways. You can't have a CD where you're calling her a queen on one track and a B on another track. I believe there would be more consistency if gangsta rappers, like all of our youth, were mentored by positive role models. That's why I respect Russell Simmons' hip-hop Summit. They are trying to give rappers some direction.

When you speak of gangsta rap, you have to deal with 50 Cent. He is popular and promoted heavily by the media because of his hard street image. He was shot nine times and was able to survive the gunshot wounds. This is the kind of image the four big media companies love to glamorize and market to our sons.

By the way, this hardness cost the brilliant rappers Tupac and Biggie their lives. Like *Boyz n the Hood,* their final scene was all about retaliation.

On "106 & Park," BET's top video show, there is a segment (Freestyle Friday) where two rappers verbally battle one another. This is the new form of playing the dozens, signifying, and cracking. But they do it within the context of rap.

People think the greatest tragedy to happen to Black people was slavery, and I definitely understand the impact slavery had on our race. As late as 1920, 90 percent of Black youth still had their fathers in the home. I believe the two current enemies of Black people, crack cocaine and gangsta rap, have been devastating to the Black family, especially our boys. We must clean both of them up. We cannot allow gangsta rappers to raise our children.

Parents, watch rap videos with your son. Point out how they promote sexism and misogyny through degrading images of Black women.

Let your son know you will be doing random searches of his rap CDs. Make sure you listen to your son's music. If the message is in the music, then we need to hear the messages our sons are listening to.

Expose your son to more conscious and gospel rap. I understand the need for music with a good beat. Young people feel that gangsta rap has a better beat than most conscious and gospel rap. Make sure the beat in the music you provide is something he can enjoy and dance to.

We need to watch "106 & Park," "Rap City: Tha Bassment," and MTV videos. I'm glad the "BET Uncut" video program was taken off the air. This was nothing but porn. Even though it was on early in the morning, our boys and girls still watched it and sometimes taped it.

People outside the Black community—in Africa, China, Europe, Australia—now define us based on gangsta rap because that's what the four major media companies are promoting. Ask your son if this is how he wants his mother, father, siblings, and himself to be represented to the world. Is this an accurate representation of the Black community? A good essay assignment for those nights when he does not have homework would be for him to write a few paragraphs describing how this image of a hard core gangsta rapper would make people in Africa or China or Europe or Australia treat him and his family.

In the next chapter, we will look at the third strongest influence on our boys, and that is television.

Chapter 20: Television/Video Games

The third strongest influence on African American youth, especially boys, is television and video games. No group watches more television than African Americans. **African American youth watch 38 hours of television per week.** The average TV viewer watches 50 minutes per day of commercials, which, taken over a lifetime, adds up to 15 years of your life spent watching commercials.

In some households, there are four people in the house and at a minimum, four televisions. Some boys have their own television in their room with a remote control and full cable. Notice that on network television the B word, S word, and D word are used, and that's tame compared to basic cable and the premium channels. On those shows there is no limit to the words that can be used. Because network television is suffering in the ratings, it is attempting to compete against cable and premium channels.

Over the past two decades, cursing has increased 95 percent on network television. In a typical hour, there's a 44 percent chance that you will see violence and sexual acts on network television, 59 percent chance on basic cable, and 85 percent chance on the premium channels. Sixty-six percent of all television shows have sexual scenes.

Seldom will you see married couples having sex on television. For some reason the networks and cable channels want to teach us that sex is primarily for individuals outside of marriage.

By the age of 13, youth have seen 100,000 acts of violence and more than 8,000 murders. This number-three influence on our youth has major implications for our sons' growth, values, and character.

Excellent research was provided in the article "Early Television Exposure and Subsequent Attention Problems in Children." Too much television viewing among toddlers leads to ADD, which leads to the prescription of Ritalin or similar drugs. It leads to stunted growth in children and accompanying social problems.

Among toddlers 1 to 3 years of age who were exposed to television every day, the authors found that every two hours of daily television viewing resulted in a 20 percent loss of attention span by the time the children turned 7.[7] Could this mean that African American toddlers risk losing 40 to 60 percent of their attention span since they watch at least twice that much television?

Not only are we seeing an increase in cursing on network television and more than 90 percent of sexual acts outside of marriage, but television is also trying to teach us to be more tolerant of homosexual relationships.

I was consulting in a preschool, and I observed two girls playing house. One girl asked the other, "Will you marry me?" A little boy came over and said, "Girls don't marry girls." They all went to the teacher and asked, "Can girls marry girls? Can boys marry boys?" The teacher was dumbfounded because she herself had been exposed to so much television that this had become the norm.

Is it true that television is shaping the values, character, and integrity of your son?

Even the powerful show, "The Wire" on HBO, which is an excellent portrayal of drug life in Baltimore, featured two homosexual couples.

This is no accident. It is not even subtle. It is becoming more blatant, and conscious, responsible parents need to address homosexuality. We cannot allow our boys to sit around watching programs like "The Wire" where Black males kiss each other.

Parents, we must reduce the tremendous impact television has on our youth, particularly our boys. The book *The Plug-in Drug* saw the problem clearly. Television is addictive. If you think that television is not a drug, try going one week without it.

Families have different strategies for dealing with television. Unfortunately, in many homes there is no strategy. There are no provisions to reduce its influence. If anything, television is used to avoid conversation among family members. This is a way to avoid giving direction to our children.

We used to say that television was the babysitter in the home, but with fathers only spending 7 minutes and mothers 34 minutes with their children, television has become the parent.

Parents believe that television can keep their sons safe and off the street. Instead of becoming the victims of "The Wire," they are watching "The Wire." We must do better.

If we are serious about reducing the impact that television has on our children, then we must look at strategies that successful parents have used to reduce that impact.

The extreme option would be no television at all. Some parents have done that and discovered some great things. They discovered they like each other. They have gotten to know each other. They play games with each other. They interact more with each other. They have Bible study together. They exercise together. They go to the health club together. They do a myriad of activities together.

Other successful families have decided to eliminate television on certain days, for example, Sunday night through Thursday night since those are school nights. They want their sons to be at their best, get more sleep, and stay focused on academics.

Some families have implemented the option of allowing one hour of television watching per day. Some have decided that the one hour has to be a family activity, parents and children watching together. Sonya Carson, with her third grade education, turned off the TV and made her son Ben read books.

Boys are smart. They'll turn off the television if you tell them to and then turn on PlayStation. Video games are a $10 billion industry, and these games are not cheap. If you thought there was violence on cable and network television, you should see some of these video games. Many are even more violent than TV. Just because your son wants the hottest game out, the game his peer group feels is the number-one game, does not mean that you should buy it. No video games should be purchased without a review by parents. If you don't feel the game is healthy for your son, don't buy it.

There are 300 channels to choose from on television, and family members often cannot agree on which program to watch as a family. So they all go to their separate rooms to watch television.

I'm out of town three or four days each week. When I get home, I would love to watch a documentary or sports event, but my wife usually wants to watch HGTV (the Home and Garden channel) or Lifetime. I have a choice: after three or four days of being out of town, I can either go to my private room and watch what I want to watch and allow television to separate me from my wife, or I can compromise and watch HGTV and Lifetime with my wife. Isn't it more important that we do things together than do things separately? We cannot allow television to separate us from each other.

Television has become a babysitter and surrogate parent. Parents need to take back the responsibility of raising their children. Television is teaching your children how to be homosexual. Television is teaching your children that sex outside of marriage is okay. Television is teaching your children that it is okay to murder someone. Television is teaching your children that cursing is acceptable.

Parents must step up to the plate and take responsibility. This is a major challenge because to take responsibility, you must begin to spend time with your children. Maybe some fathers are okay with 7 minutes and some mothers are okay with 34 minutes. If you think that's okay, then understand that you will not be an influence in your son's life.

Reducing the influence of television on your son is not going to be easy. Television is the third strongest presence in your son's life because media executives were strategic and effective in reaching that position. If you are going to usurp television's impact, you will need a game plan, a strategy, commitment, and determination. If you are not willing to do that, you will have to accept the consequences.

In the next chapter, we will look at sports. It has a tremendous influence on our youth.

Chapter 21: Sports

If we provided daily gym in schools and allowed boys to release their energy, I believe special education referrals would be reduced.

Sports play a major role in the lives of African American males. There is a difference between playing alley ball and structured ball with a coach. A mistake parents sometimes make is to make it optional for their sons to be involved in various programs.

Many boys would rather run and gun. They don't want to submit to a program of discipline, teamwork, organizational skills, structure, and responsibility. They would rather play alley ball with their friends. In alley ball, you play whenever, pass the ball whenever, play defense whenever, hustle whenever, and play as long as you want.

There are many benefits to playing structured sports. Structured sports require discipline, time management, organizational skills, and teamwork. One of the most important benefits of sports, especially for the 68 percent of African American males who do not have a father in the home, is that the coach is a surrogate father. Many of our boys are being reared by coaches.

The most important male in many boys' lives is his coach. Just as there are five types of teachers, there are various types of coaches. Not all coaches are the same. Furthermore, a college may be a powerhouse in sports, but the athletes' graduation rates are abysmal. College athletes who lack discipline are often in the news for their numerous illegal and wild activities, yet the school and coaching program allow them to continue to play.

The best coaches have strong expertise in their sport, and they develop character in their athletes. Two excellent examples are the late Eddie Robinson, the former football coach at Grambling University, and my coach, the late Gerald Richards. Eddie Robinson coached at Grambling for more than 50 years.

No football coach produced more NFL players than Robinson. Although more than 200 African American males went to the NFL because of Eddie Robinson, that was not his greatest accomplishment. His claim to fame is that he produced more than 3,000 graduates. Thanks to Eddie Robinson, more than 3,000 African American males walked the aisle to receive their degrees.

Reading this great man's autobiography, I was struck by the fact that winning was second in importance to him. Every time he looked at one of his ballplayers, he looked at a potential mate for his daughter. He wanted his young men to have the same type of character he was looking for in a son-in-law. Eddie Robinson had thousands of sons.

My own track coach, the late Gerald Richards, was a brilliant coach, and we won several city and state championships. However, that was not his greatest achievement. He taught us discipline and character. He would have us run from 3:00 pm until 6:00 pm almost every day. At 6:00 he would ask us if we were tired. We were always exhausted. Then he'd say, "Now the workout will begin." Anybody can run when they're fresh, but can you run when you're tired?

He taught me that lesson 40 years ago, and I still use it today, especially when I'm on the lecture circuit in February and speaking almost every day. A coach's lessons can last a lifetime.

Teachers in Chicago would often go on strike, so our school year would start late. But not the track season. Coach Richards would say, "I don't care if we're on strike or not. I expect you to be on the track at 3:00 pm. I don't want you to be behind when the season begins." Since then I've wondered why teachers on strike don't volunteer to teach reading or math at the local library and churches if they are so concerned about students getting behind. You don't mind giving 110 percent to your coach when you see your coach is giving 110 percent to you.

Once we lost to a White team in a cross-country race. There's a rumor that African Americans are good in the sprints and Whites are better in the long-distance races. Ironically,

Africans from the continent are winning the marathons, 10,000 meters, 5,000 meters, and 1,500 meters. Could it be that Africans on the continent are taught to run long distance while Africans in the U.S. are taught to run sprints?

Charles Murray, it has nothing to do with genetics and everything to do with expectations and time on task.

When we lost to the White team, Gerald Richards was furious. He took us back to our high school and at around 8:00 that night had us run 48 quarter mile sprints until almost midnight. He told us emphatically, "You better not ever lose to another White team in cross-country again." Believe me, we did not.

Too many of our boys have too much idle time. Involvement in sports can fix that. One barometer of your son's success is the amount of idle time he has. High school lets out as early as 2:00 or 3:00 in the afternoon, which means our boys are on the street from 3:00 pm until curfew, and sometimes they violate curfew. They come in even later on the weekend.

Can you imagine, some boys are hanging out from 3:00 to 6:00 pm—that's 7 hours on weekdays—and from noon to midnight, 12 hours, on Saturday and Sunday. Our boys have 35 hours of idle time during the week and 24 hours on the weekends. That's 59 hours of idle time per week that could be spent doing something constructive.

Successful parents have done a good job at reducing idle time. Some parents allow their sons no idle time. When I was in high school, we had to run from 3:00 to 6:00 pm. Coach then drove us home by 7:30 pm. Then I'd do my homework and eat dinner. We were so tired, we'd go to bed. On Saturday, we had track meets, and at my house, we went to church on Sunday. When I was with my grandparents in Texas, there was Sunday school, church, and Sunday evening service. It is difficult to get in trouble with a schedule like that.

Another benefit to structured sports was that it gave me little opportunity, if any, to be in a gang. Even gangs have a sense of order and character about them. Once a gang member approached me and saw that I was a track runner. He simply said, "Keep running. As long as you keep running, you won't have a problem with us." That might have encouraged me to run faster.

Involvement in sports reduces the use of drugs, smoking, and drinking. Athletes want to perform at their highest level, and for the most part they realize that engaging in risky behaviors will only hurt their performance.

However, sports is not foolproof. I'm concerned about the many professional ball players in the NBA and NFL (sometimes called the National Felon League) who are suspended from play because of their illegal and wild activities off the field and court. Clearly, they do not appreciate the privilege of playing in the NBA and NFL.

One of the benefits of running track is that there is a cross-country indoor and outdoor season. Literally, we were running from September through June. In other sports, like football, athletes play from September through November. If they are not playing another sport, they have almost a half a year to get in trouble with drugs, smoking, and drinking.

Sports involvement will keep your sons in shape and also prevent obesity. In the excellent book *Strength for Their Journey,* Robert Johnson discusses the relationship between watching television and being overweight. Listed below are the findings of his research.[8]

Hours of TV Watched Daily	% of Kids Who Are Overweight
0-2	12
2-3	23
3-4	28
4-5	30
5+	33

Sports

More than one-third of America's children are either over-weight or obese. Many schools offer physical education only once or twice a week at the elementary level.

If our boys understand the importance of sports, they will always see themselves as athletes. I'm now in my 50s, and I still see myself as an athlete. I'm concerned about males who were stars in high school and college and later became more than 100 pounds overweight and now can barely touch their toes—and they haven't touched a ball in years.

If you appreciate sports and all its benefits, you will be an athlete for life. You may change your sport from basketball to swimming, golf, or tennis, but you will always be an athlete. You'll do whatever you can to work on your stomach and keep your heart rate strong.

Once an athlete, always an athlete. We need to teach that to our sons.

We need to teach our sons that there are more sports than just basketball and football. For Black boys there is only one sport, and that is basketball. In the excellent book *Hooked on Hoops: Understanding Black Youths' Blind Devotion to Basketball,* author Kevin McNutt talks about the tremendous obsession Black youth have with basketball. Sixty-six percent of African American males believe they are going to be a pro in the NBA. Let me clear things up a bit.

- One million males have a desire to go pro in the NBA.
- Only 400,000 make the high school team.
- 4,000 make the college team.
- 35 make the NBA.
- 7 start.
- Average NBA career: four years.

Can you imagine, we have one million African American males looking for seven full-time jobs that last only four years. We need to expand our boys' horizons. Parents, expose your son to golf, swimming, tennis, baseball, wrestling, and soccer. Many high schools struggle to fill the team positions in these sports.

171

Jackie Robinson would be disappointed to find out that only 8 percent of major league baseball players are African American. It used to be as high as 33 percent.

Boys need to understand the mathematics of sports. In the NBA there are only 12 positions on approximately 30 teams, totaling 360 slots.

In the NFL there are 45 positions and 30 teams, or 1,350 slots.

In baseball, there are 25 positions and 30 teams, or 750 slots.

Do the math. In baseball, if you can field a ground ball and bat .250, you'll be paid $1 million per year in the major leagues. Left-handed relief pitchers face only one or two batters every second or third day; they are paid more than $1 million per year. By the way, the average career of a baseball player is seven years.

Richard Williams, father of Venus and Serena, found out that top tennis players can earn $1 million in one tournament. He decided he needed to teach his daughters how to play tennis, and he did exactly that.

Boys need to know about James Blake, who earned more than $15 million a year playing tennis. Tiger Woods earns more than $100 million per year playing golf. Tiger does not get hit. He does not have any knee or ankle injuries. This is very different from basketball and football, which are high-contact sports. We need to expand our boys' horizons.

Ask your son if he can name 20 African American ball players in the NBA with a college degree. This is important because 75 percent of African American college ball players do not graduate. Parents need to be careful about where their sons go to college to play. Look for a 70 percent or greater graduation rate among athletes.

I must mention the former coach of Georgetown University, John Thompson, and the great work his son, John Thompson, Jr., is doing presently. John Thompson negotiated at Georgetown that if ball players like Patrick Ewing can bring $12 million per year to the school in TV contracts, the least the school can do is provide a five-year contract, tutors in the athletes' hotel rooms and airplanes when they played out of town, and tutors in their dormitories.

The Black peer group says that Blacks play basketball and football, and Whites swim, wrestle, and play tennis and golf. I'm concerned about the Black peer group encouraging 200 ball players to try out for 12 slots on the high school basketball team but discouraging any African American male from participating in science fairs and debate and spelling bee contests. Our athletes should participate in both sports and academics.

Arthur Ashe, the late, great tennis player, also valued academics. David Robinson, the former NBA star for the San Antonio Spurs, was a great athlete and a scholar in the Navy. He delayed his NBA career to honor a promise to give several years to the Navy as an officer.

Your son needs to read about A.C. Green, the former star for the Los Angeles Lakers. This brilliant ball player did not take advantage of women. When teammate Magic Johnson was involved with numerous women, A.C. Green made a vow to the Lord: no sex until marriage. Can you imagine how many women were attracted to A.C. Green? But he kept his morals and character.

Thank God the story does not end with all the women Magic Johnson had in his hotel room. Magic had to retire from the NBA when he was diagnosed HIV positive. However, he knew he was more than just a basketball player. Magic Johnson is now one of the most astute businessmen in the world. He's earning far more money outside of sports than he ever made inside. Parents, if your son is a gifted athlete, make sure his sport does not define him. Expose him to other arenas, and by all means, make sure he's doing his homework and excelling in all of his classes.

Life is 10 percent what happens to you and 90 percent how you respond to it. When Magic was diagnosed HIV positive, he could have thrown in the towel. He could have given up on himself. He could have let his body go and ignored all medical advice. He could have chosen to rest on his laurels and not pursued another career. Instead, Magic Johnson has stayed in shape and continues to play ball. He understands that he's an athlete for life. In addition, he owns numerous franchises and is involved in a myriad of activities in the Black economic community.

Your son should read about the life of Muhammad Ali. He was far more than a boxer. Drafted by the Army, Ali refused to serve in Vietnam because he considered it an unjust war. He said, "Man, I ain't got no quarrel with them Vietcong." He refused to go to war, he refused a safe Army job, and he even refused to go to Canada, where many war resisters were hiding. As a result, Muhammad Ali's championship title was taken from him, and he was sentenced to five years in prison (which was overturned on appeal). That's character. That's integrity.

Muhammad Ali understood the importance of Black history and culture. If only we had more wealthy athletes who were grounded in Black history and culture.

Your son should read about what Stephon Marbury, the brilliant guard for the New York Knicks, has done for the shoe industry. He puts pressure on Michael Jordan and LeBron James to deal with the fact that the shoes made overseas for less than $3 are sold in the U.S. for more than $100. Stephon Marbury has come out with his own shoe that sells for less than $15. I encourage you to buy your sons these shoes, but more importantly, help them understand the lesson that Stephon Marbury is trying to teach.

Since 86 percent of the NBA but only 2 percent of engineers and doctors are African American , some parents have begun to emphasize academics over athletics. Some have literally eliminated sports. But remember, the pecking order in the Black male peer group is powerful. The peer group does not value AP classes. It does value how well your son can dunk a basketball, throw a football, hit a baseball, and run around a track. Parents need to be aware of the pecking order and its impact on our boys' self-esteem.

A great benefit of sports is that going to college is expected and highly anticipated among the athletes. When I ran track as a freshman, I would listen to the juniors and seniors talk about the colleges they planned to attend. As I matriculated through school, I understood that I too would be going to college. The first time many boys hear about college is when they begin playing on a team.

If your son does well in his sport, he could receive a college scholarship. Proposition 48, 42, 14, and 16 require that students earn a certain GPA and score a certain number on the ACT and SAT to be eligible to play. This has put more pressure on coaches to make sure their athletes do well academically. The better coaches insist on reviewing report cards on a quarterly basis, and they confer with their athletes' teachers. It is unfortunate that some coaches are more involved in their athletes' academic experience than the parents.

Some athletes would say that GIRLS are the biggest benefit of sports. Girls gravitate to athletes. Male-female relationships are extremely important and have a major impact on male self-esteem. It is a nice feeling to be a star athlete and receive a lot of attention from the girls.

It is troublesome that our boys receive such little support from their parents in the sports arena. Have you ever attended a basketball or football game and counted the number of African American parents in attendance? Our boys deserve our support. Not only must we monitor their teachers and evening homework sessions but they need us to encourage them in their pursuit of sports. When I ran track, my father worked at the post office from 3:00 to 11:00 pm. Our track meets were usually around 4:00 pm. My father would negotiate with his boss to take his lunch and breaks around my track meets. I was one of the few athletes who had parents at those meets. In fact, my father became a surrogate father for many of my teammates.

Before closing, I would be remiss if I didn't discuss NBA wannabes. There are one million young males looking for seven full-time jobs that last only four years. What about the 999,993 African American males who had a desire to go pro, who thought they were going pro, but unfortunately did not make it? What are they doing now?

Do you know how many NBA wannabes are washing dishes in restaurants? They're still talking a good game in the barbershops about the good old days when they were one step away from being drafted in the NBA.

Do you know how sad it is to hear stories from NBA wannabes? They love to talk about the good old days. There are consequences to putting all of your hopes into a profession where the odds are stacked against you—one million to seven.

In the next chapter, we will look at sexuality.

Chapter 22: Sexuality

This is a life and death chapter. Let's begin with a look at the American sexual landscape.

- African Americans represent only 12 percent of the U.S. population, but 43 percent of all males in America with AIDS are African American.
- Fifty-six million Americans have an STD (sexually transmitted disease).
- The chlamydia rate for Black teens ages 15 to 19 is seven times higher than the rate for White teens and three times higher than the Hispanic teen rate.
- Black teens account for 78 percent of all cases of gonorrhea among adolescents between ages 15 and 19.
- The rate of gonorrhea infection is two-thirds as high in Black males as it is in Black females.
- African American males in the 15-to-19-year-old category have a gonorrhea rate that is 52 times higher than the rate for 15-to-19-year-old White males.
- Black teens account for 81 percent of all cases of syphilis among adolescents ages 15 to 19.[9]

I speak to thousands of young people nationwide who, when I share these statistics, tell me they will not catch anything. Many tell me they are virgins. I ask them, "But are you having oral sex?" Most say yes.

How unfortunate that many of our youth think that oral sex is not sex. **Oral sex can kill you.**

This foolishness began when former President Bill Clinton made that infamous statement, "I did not have sex with that woman." Young people think that oral sex is not sex.

There's an old saying, "Boys will be boys." That's true. Boys will be boys—if you let them. Remember, there's a distinction between being a male, a boy, and a man. Boys like to play with cars, trucks, and balls. Older boys like to play with women, children, and sex.

When we think virgin and teen pregnancy, we think "female." How unfortunate that most teen pregnancy programs counsel females and not males. Almost 90 percent of teen pregnancy programs focus on females, and yet the reality is that both genders are equally involved.

When we think of a person taking an oath of abstinence or virginity like A.C. Green, we think "female." Is it not possible for your son to at least know about this option, that he can abstain from sex until marriage?

Why do we think female parts are more valuable than male parts?

Why does our society encourage girls to keep their legs closed, but it's okay for a male to show any and everything?

My parents taught me that my parts are just as valuable as hers and that she should want me as much as I want her. Parents (especially mothers), even if you feel uncomfortable talking to your son about sex, you must talk about it, and you must start early. The burden of teaching sex education should not fall on schools or the church. It should start at home. Unfortunately, parents have relinquished this responsibility.

If you wait until your son is 16 or 18, there's a good chance he will say, "Oh, sex? What do you want to know?" Our boys think they know more than we do.

In fact, boys are becoming sexually active as early as 9 years old while their first exposure to sex education may come when they are 16 or 18. There's truly a generational gap here that we need to close.

Listed below is a brief chronology of our boys' growth and development.

- At age 8, the boy becomes interested in sex.
- At 9, the boy becomes very private about his body, especially with his mother.
- At 10, erections occur frequently.
- At 11, about 50 percent or more of all boys will masturbate.
- At 12, boys begin to ejaculate.

Parents need to teach their sons about the significance of these changes. Boys need to know about the changes their female peers are experiencing as well.

In an excellent study done by Dr. Cohen, the Black Youth Project, 31 percent of African American youth reported that at the age of 16 they had yet to receive any sex education from home, school, or church. There's a terrible trick being played on our youth. The trick involves the body, the mind, and the economy.

Our children are maturing faster than ever before, thanks to the large amount of cow's milk and red meat our children are consuming. Cow's milk and red meat are filled with hormones. As a result, today's children have overdeveloped bodies. When I speak at high schools, I can't tell the difference between the girls and the adult female teachers. Nor can I distinguish between the high school boys and the adult male teachers.

The second part of the trick is that the minds of our children are overexposed. This generation has seen more sexual acts than any other before.

- Fifty-six percent of all prime time network television shows and more than 90 percent of cable and premium channels have sexual scenes.
- Ninety percent of sexual scenes on television take place outside of marriage.
- Ten percent of sexual scenes on television involve adolescents.
- Nine percent of sexual scenes on television involve homosexuals.
- For some strange reason, contraceptives, STDs, and AIDS are seldom presented as the consequences of this behavior.

The overdeveloped bodies of our youth are physically ready for sex and procreation. They see more than 50,000 sexual scenes by age 18, 90 percent of which take place outside of marriage. A tremendous amount of pressure has been placed on our youth to have sex, yet the economy says they must wait.

In the 1920s, a 15-year-old boy could propose to a 15-year-old girl. They could get married and at age 16 have their first child. They worked on a farm, and they raised their children.

In 1960, an 18-year-old male could propose to an 18-year-old female. They could give birth to a child at age 19. They worked in a factory, and they raised their children.

We now live in the 21st century, the Information Economy. Our children's overdeveloped bodies and overexposed minds are ready for sex as early as 8 years old, but they cannot financially provide for their children. They know they should wait until they are self-sufficient, but the pressure to have sex is just too great. Sex is the dominant thought on the minds of our youth. Gangsta rap, television, and peer pressure have made sure of that.

So our children are having sex and making babies and giving them to grandparents to be reared because they cannot provide for their children.

A terrible trick has been played on our youth, but we can turn the evil tide around. First, reduce or eliminate the amount of cow's milk and red meat your son consumes. Second, reduce the amount of television he is watching. When he watches, watch it with him. As he watches sexual scenes, tell him that 56 million Americans have an STD and that 43 percent of all HIV-positive males are African American, since for some strange reason television doesn't provide this information.

The Rand Corporation researched the impact gangsta rap lyrics have on sexual activity. Youth that listen regularly to gangsta rap lyrics become sexually involved two years earlier than those youth who do not.[10] In those negative findings lies a solution. We need to either limit or eliminate our children's exposure to gangsta rap, or we need to turn gangsta rap tunes into a lesson. What are the sexual consequences of listening to this music?

The number one influence on youth is peer pressure. The Black male peer group exerts tremendous pressure to be sexually active. A teenage male is at the low end of the pecking order if he has not had sex. It's almost like part of the school uniform for every male to have a condom in his wallet. Even if they have not become sexually active, many males feel pressured to have a condom in their wallet.

The male peer group is very demanding. At some point they not only want you to have a condom in your wallet, they want you to prove you actually used it and tell with whom. Parents, have you checked your son's wallet lately?

One parent told me that her form of sex education went like this: "I told my son, 'You'd better not bring home a baby, and here's a box of condoms to make sure you don't.' " End of lesson. She said the boy must have really learned the lesson well because less than 30 days later, he was back asking for another box of condoms, and there are 30 in a box.

Sex today is life threatening. The male peer group decides how boys must think about females and sex. Unfortunately, their feelings toward women are inspired by gangsta rap and television. Let's now discuss how gangsta rap lyrics and videos promote misogyny and sexism.

Are you raising a sexist son?

Does your son have misogynistic tendencies?

One of every four Black women is raped, not by White men but Black men. Has your son ever raped a female?

Has your son ever called a female a B or an H? Believe me, Don Imus was simply the tip of the iceberg.

Many males see females as objects to conquer. The male peer group bets on how long it will take to have sex with a female. We need more Eddie Robinsons to teach males that females should be treated like queens, not B's and H's.

The following are only a few sexist words some males use to describe females.

- A piece
- I'm going to knock it out.
- I'm going to screw her.
- I'm going to jam it.

- I'm going to bang it.
- I'm going to stain her.
- I'm going to hit it.
- The F word.

God did not intend for these words to describe sex, one of His greatest gifts.

Has your son ever been in a "train," where several males (not men) take sexual advantage of a female one after another? They collectively have sex with her.

The second most important decision young males will make, after putting God first in their lives, is the selection of a mate. Have you taught your son how to select the right mate? Does your son know how to date? Does he know how to honor women? Have you taught him to open doors for females? To avoid pre-marital sex, have you encouraged group dating? Time limits? Have you met her parents?

The divorce rate in Black America is close to 70 percent. Divorce is costly. Many a Black male will tell you he may never marry again. He may never have children again after going through child support for the first time. Your son needs to know how important this decision is. This decision could cost him one-fourth to one-third of his income. It cost Michael Jordan more than $150 million.

Is your son willing to let another man give direction to his children?

Is your son prepared to have his children reared in two different households?

There is a science to selecting the right mate. In 2 Corinthians 6:14, Paul talks about being equally yoked. You need to teach your son what it means to be equally yoked. Your son should not believe that opposites attract. He should choose a mate with similar values, i.e. goals, work ethic.

Lack of communication is one of the major reasons for divorce. Your son should marry his best friend and not just his lover. Tell him he shouldn't make his decision purely based on looks. Even Halle Berry's looks couldn't keep her marriage together.

Your son needs to find a mate with whom he can share his most intimate secrets. He must trust her enough to open the lines of communication.

Have you heard people say, "Ain't nothing going on. We're just friends." How unfortunate. That should have been the mate, the one who was your best friend.

Your son should not marry without premarital counseling. Premarital counseling should take at least one year. Also, a couple should date one year before entering premarital counseling.

Parents, talk to your son about the woman he plans to marry. Many parents keep quiet because they feel their son will not listen anyway, and they do not want to accelerate the decision.

Ideally, you should sit down with your son at age 13 and create a premarital contract for him to sign. The contract would say that your son cannot get married without your input. He has to marry his best friend. They have to date a minimum of one year. They must have premarital counseling for one year. Have your son sign the contract at age 13. Show him the contract at age 21 or whenever he begins to think about marriage.

Will your son be a sperm donor, which takes 18 seconds, or will he be a daddy, which will take a minimum of 18 years? The ball is in your court, parents.

Do you see your son as a future husband and father, or do you see him as simply a replacement for your husband who did not stay? Some mothers raise their daughters and love their sons. Some mothers like having their 40-year-old son stay at home. He can cut the grass, empty the garbage, and do minor repairs around the house. But your son is not yours, and the sooner you see your 9-year-old son as someone's husband, someone's father, the better both of your lives will be.

You need to teach your son to be a gentleman. He needs to open the door for you. He needs to respect you like a queen. If I were advising a female, I would tell her, "If you really want to find out about your future mate, look at how he treats his mother. That's a good indicator of how he's going to treat you."

Since this book is about sons, let's reverse the question. Mothers, how does your son treat you?

Are you raising a sexist son?

Are you raising a son with misogynistic tendencies?

Does he see women as objects to be conquered, or does he see them as queens to be revered and respected?

Would your son ever physically or emotionally abuse a female?

How you answer those questions will determine the future of your son.

In the next chapter we will look at the safety of your sons.

Chapter 23: Safety/Gangs/Drugs

The greatest challenge for our boys is not learning algebra, geometry, or trigonometry. It's not learning biology, chemistry, or physics. Their greatest challenge is the five-block walk from home to school without being beaten up.

It is a shame what our boys must endure in many neighborhoods as they walk and take the bus to school. I run numerous mentoring and rites of passage programs nationwide. One year, one of my young men was denied admission into one of the select magnet schools in the city. I wrote letters protesting the Board's decision because I felt this particular young man deserved entrance into the program. I did not feel these special magnet schools should be reserved for only a few White students.

Eventually the young man was accepted into one of the schools. When I told him the good news, he thanked me, then asked, "Where exactly is the school?" He had already begun to calculate how many neighborhoods, gangs, trials, and fights he would have to withstand to get from point A to point B.

It's tragic what our boys are experiencing. How many times have we heard of boys being killed when all they were doing was riding their bikes or walking on the block? There have been horror stories of boys in their own homes, not even close to a window, being shot by stray bullets.

While writing this book, Blair Holt, a graduating high school senior, was gunned down on a Chicago bus by a 16-year-old Black male drop out. His parents, a father who works in the gangs unit of the Chicago Police Department, and his mother, a captain in the Fire Department, dropped him off at school daily. Their schedules prevented them from picking him up. Blair had been accepted in college. The gunman was attempting to shoot someone else. Blair blocked the bullet from hitting a female friend sitting next to him.

Many parents move to racist neighborhoods with insensitive teachers for the sole purpose of keeping their sons safe. How many Blairs do we have to lose? He was a future college graduate, possible husband and father that the Black community will never experience. His shooter was illiterate, a drop out, fatherless, unsaved, and possessed a gun. That is a dangerous combination.

Safety is a priority for parents, and many make the decision to move to a safer environment. They struggle to move to areas that are often beyond their financial means. While this decision may address physical safety, it does not address emotional and academic safety because now the child is a potential victim of what Malcolm Little experienced with his racist teacher. Although these boys are no longer threatened by gangs in the inner city, they are now in real danger of a highly sophisticated gang in schools that wants to place them in special education.

I sympathize with the dilemma these families face. Children need to live and grow and play and learn in nurturing environments, and that includes more than just personal safety. Our boys need to see grass. They should be able to play outside without worrying about being hit by a car or a stray bullet. I have observed our children in many different settings: hanging on the corner in the inner city, going on nature walks with Cub Scouts and Boy Scouts, reading about African history in rites of passage and mentoring classes, riding a bike with friends in the suburbs, and just running in grassy fields without any worry or concern. While our boys can learn in any type of environment, some settings are more nurturing than others. It is hard to learn algebra and physics when you're worried about getting jumped when the bell rings. On the other hand, learning is easier when the entire village is geared to that purpose, when even the peer group is competitive academically. That's the ideal, and every boy deserves to have that experience.

Parents who are not financially able to move from crime-ridden neighborhoods but who are equally anxious about their sons' safety simply make them stay in the house. Dr. Raymond Winbush, the brilliant professor who wrote *The Warrior Method: A Program for Rearing Black Boys*, believes our boys are warriors. It is difficult keeping the warrior confined for long periods of time, from 3:00 to 10:00 pm Monday through

Friday and from sun up to sun down Saturday and Sunday. I understand the dilemma, but having boys stay in the house all day every day is not healthy. Something will have to give.

Bullying

Ninety percent of our children are bullied, but parents never know because their sons stay silent about what they are enduring. In the book *Raising Boys,* Steve Biddulph provides the following warning signs that your son may be the victim of bullying:

- Physical signs (unexplained bruises, scratches, and cuts)
- Damage to clothes or belongings
- Stress-caused illnesses (unexplained pain, headaches, and stomach aches)
- Fearful behavior (fear of walking to school, deciding to take different routes at the last minute, asking to be driven)
- Decline in quality of school work
- Coming home hungry (bag lunch and lunch money stolen)
- Asking for or stealing money (to pay the bully)
- Having few friends (rarely being invited to parties)
- Changes in behavior (withdrawn, stammering, moody, irritable, upset, unhappy, tearful, or distressed)
- Not eating
- Attempting suicide or hinting at suicide
- Anxiety (bedwetting, nail biting, fearfulness, not sleeping, crying out in sleep)
- Refusal to say what is wrong
- Giving improbable excuses for any of the above[11]

Martial arts and other self-defense arts are important for boys to master. You're low on the pecking order if you cannot defend yourself and if you allow bullies to take advantage of you.

When I was growing up there was a bully who was messing with me. I was concerned because he had many brothers. I feared that if I fought the bully, his brothers would step in. My father told me that if I didn't fight the bully, I would get two whippings: one from the bully and one from him. I'm sure many mothers would have thought that was cruel. That's why God gave children two parents; they have different perspectives on various issues. I'm not saying that fathers are always right, but they do have a different perspective from women who haven't gone through male experiences.

Before he was a man, he was a boy. My father experienced some of the same incidents that I experienced growing up. That cannot be true for mothers.

The beauty of this story is that I fought the bully that day, and I won. Fortunately, his brothers did not jump in. In fact, his brothers said, "We're glad you did it. He was getting on our nerves, too."

Parents, help your son develop confidence in his ability to defend himself against anyone, especially bullies. It is suicidal for you to raise your son, especially in certain neighborhoods, without the ability to defend himself. You must not raise a punk. You must not raise a sissy. You must not raise a wimp. Raise a man who is fully capable of defending himself and his loved ones. Enroll your son in boxing, martial arts, and other self-defense classes.

As if self-defense isn't challenging enough, our boys must contend with the different cultural values regarding fighting. In school, the rule is that if someone hits you, tell the teacher. In Black culture, especially Black male culture, if someone hits you, hit him back.

This creates a tremendous amount of pressure on African American males. If they tell, the adult may not be able to protect them. Boys say they have tried telling, but the adult couldn't (or wouldn't) protect them. As soon as the school day ended and they had to walk home, there was nothing the adult could do since they were off school grounds. So boys have to take matters into their own hands.

In the Black community there is a disdain for **snitching**. We do not trust anyone in authority: school personnel, the police, the justice department. The stop snitching movement began in Boston in 1992 and was promoted by the now infamous T-shirts. The shirts were originally a promotional item for the rapper Tangg. Parents have been clueless about the significance of the stop snitching campaign.

The stop snitching campaign gained national attention in late 2004 in Baltimore, Maryland, where a DVD released by Rodney Thomas titled "Stop Snitching" began to circulate. NBA star Carmelo Anthony, a former Baltimore resident, appeared in the video. As the DVD spread across the country, promotional T-shirts became popular in urban youth fashion. The shirts typically show a stop sign emblazoned with the words Stop Snitching. Some shirts have bullet holes, implying that snitches will be shot. The shirts have been more widely circulated than the original DVD. Another T-shirt says I'll Never Tell.

Lil' Kim, in one of her rap CDs, said, "Under pressure I'll lie for you, I'll die for you." She went to federal prison in Philadelphia for refusing to tell a grand jury what she knew about some friends who were involved in a shooting.

In a well-known interview in *XXL* magazine, Immortal Technique contended that Blacks and Latinos should not snitch until police officers take responsibility for their own actions and inform on each other when brutality is committed against members of their community.

In rap culture, it is important to appear hard. Many rappers feel that adhering to the no-snitching code maintains their image and reputation and helps increase record sales.

Our boys are not safe because they live in neighborhoods that are not controlled by men. They live in neighborhoods controlled by 12-to-19-year-old males. Listed below are some of the many reasons why our sons join gangs.

Gangs are one of the unfortunate realities negatively impacting teen life. Why do young people join gangs?

1. Money. Many youth join gangs to make fast money. Financially disadvantaged young people look for ways to buy expensive starter jackets, tennis shoes, and electronic equipment. They'd rather participate in one drug deal and make enough money to buy something than spend a full month working at a fast-food restaurant.

2. Power. Gangs promise power to youth who feel powerless over their lives. Although power offers a false sense of security, they have no other healthy sources for support.

3. Identity. Many youth are desperately searching for a place to belong. Gangs accept youth who don't feel loved or accepted by parents, adults, or school. Gang identity also offers members guidelines on how to act and dress.

4. Protection. Many youth feel forced to join a gang for protection from other gangs, especially in the inner city. The gang provides a false sense of protection from the law.

5. Fun. Gangs provide activities and a social life. Many youth enjoy living on the edge and participating in dangerous activities. What first appears to be fun usually has serious consequences.

6. Intimidation. Many youth join gangs because of fear, threats, and intimidation from other gang members or bullies. Young people may want to join a gang to appear tough or more acceptable.

7. Shock. If young people aren't getting positive attention from parents, joining a gang certainly provides lots of negative attention. Youth who are angry at a parent may join a gang to shock them or to be defiant.

8. Romance. Many young people don't know what gangs are really about and have a misguided sense of romance about them. They might think they can join the gang for fun and get out whenever they wish. They might also believe that joining a gang will not involve them in violence and criminal activity.

9. Family Involvement. Family members in gangs often recruit other family members. Young people who grow up with a parent involved in a gang are at extreme risk of joining a gang. Gang involvement becomes a way of life for some families.

10. Low Self-Esteem. Youth who don't feel good about themselves are more vulnerable, and they will seek out ways to feel accepted. If healthy options aren't available, they may look to gangs for support.

11. Academic Problems. Young people who do not find success at school may see no hope or future for themselves in education. Many don't believe they could ever get a good job or go to college, so they look for other alternatives.

It used to be that a person got out of a gang and grew up. He got a real job to take care of his family. Now, gang members are older; some are in their 40s and 50s. Crack cocaine has a lot to do with this unfortunate reality. I used to believe the greatest tragedy to affect the Black community was slavery until I researched crack cocaine.

During slavery, the mother was sold to a plantation in one state, the father to another, and the children to yet another. But after slavery, they went looking for each other. We once believed that nothing could separate African American parents from their children.

There is now something that can separate parents from their children. This could be Satan's greatest trick. It's crack cocaine. It can make mothers, fathers, and children do tricks. It can make parents sell their children for another hit of the drug.

In 1980, one of every ten African American males was involved with the penal system. With the onslaught of crack cocaine in our neighborhoods, now one of every three African American males is involved with the penal system. By 2020, it is projected that two of every three will be involved.

Do you know of any industry that pays better than crack cocaine?

Do you think our boys will listen to a teacher? At some point they will stand up and say, "How much money do you make? I make that in a day." A 9-year-old boy can earn enough crack money in one day to buy a pair of Michael Jordan gym shoes. A paper route cannot compete with that. Unfortunately, boys think short term, not long term. They don't realize that **drug dealers don't retire**. Your son needs to know the three things that happen to drug dealers: they get addicted to the drug they sell, they go to jail, or they die.

When I speak to young people I ask them, "Will you make more money as a drug dealer or a school teacher?" They always say they can make more money as a drug dealer. Initially I agree with them. School teachers make $100 to $400 per day; drug dealers, on their best days, can earn up to $10,000. At this point, the class is laughing at teachers. Then I show them the following chart.

Drug Dealer: Best day: $10,000
Average month: $700
Average annual salary: $8,400
Average career: $84,000 (10 years)
Outcome: Addiction, jail, or death

Teachers: New teachers: $25,000 annually
Experienced teachers (10+ years): $50,000 annually
Average career: $50,000 x 40 years = $2,000,000
Outcome: Retired and living well

Our boys think short term because the adults in their lives are not giving them long-term aspirations. Occasionally I am driven to speaking engagements in a limousine. The first question I hear from youth is, "Are you a ball player? A rapper? A drug dealer?" The assumption is if you ride in a limousine, you must be one of the three. We need to expose our boys to successful African American male role models who are doing well financially in careers outside of the NBA, rap, or drugs.

Seventy-four percent of all drug users are White, but more than 70 percent of those convicted for possession are Black and Hispanic. If there is a war on drugs, shouldn't we spend more time investigating the White community than Blacks and

Hispanics since the problem is more prevalent with Whites?

We also need to write our congressperson to eradicate the 100:1 discrepancy between cocaine and crack convictions. Currently, it takes 500 grams of cocaine to receive a mandatory sentence, but only 5 grams of crack. Why is it that possession of 499 grams of cocaine gets you a mere slap on the wrist and a homework assignment, but possession of 5 grams of crack will land you a mandatory sentence? We need to protest this entrenched, systemic racism. What would happen if Black America refused to go to work today? What would happen if we refused to send our children to school until this 100:1 ratio was corrected?

Seventy percent of all inmates are in prison because of crack cocaine. This is unacceptable. Black leadership needs to make sure this is number one on their agenda.

Beyond crack cocaine, why is there so much violence in the Black community? How can there be so much violence with 85,000 churches in Black America, sometimes three or four on a block? With all these churches, our communities should be the safest in the country, but they are not.

Why is there so much violence in the Black community? You can answer that question with this one: Why do Black males hate themselves?

I love using videos with young people because they are so visually oriented. In the closing scene of the movie *Juice,* Tupac says, as he points a gun at the head of his adversary, "Now you know what I'm going to do to you because you know what I think of myself."

Why do Black males hate themselves?

Why do boys fight each other?

- Because they hate themselves.
- They fight people of their race because they hate their race.
- They want attention.

193

- The angriest boy really wants a hug and some praise.
- That is how they see their peers and family resolve conflict.
- They have low self-esteem because they either do not know God and their
  history or have not identified their talents and purpose in life.
- They think manhood is physical rather than mental and spiritual.
- The influence of television, video games, gangs, and rap music.
- They are frustrated because they have not experienced academic success.
- They feel fighting is their best and only strength.
- They are mad either because they are poor, have an absent father, and/or live in a slum neighborhood.
- They do not know their history, they hate their present conditions, and they do not feel confident about their future.
- Because of weak teachers and parents.
- They have not experienced a caring, intellectually sound, spirit-filled man.

Many of our boys have a chip on their shoulder. They literally walk to school daring someone to knock the chip off their shoulder so they can fight. Does your child have a chip on his shoulder?

Is your son angry?

Does your son hate himself?

Does your son know how to control his anger?

Boys do not know how to control their anger. Men do. We must teach our sons to take the chip off their shoulder. We must teach them how to manage their anger. Listed below are strategies to help manage anger.

- Take five deep breaths.
- Count from 1 to 100.

- Say "Jesus" five times.
- Say "I will bless the Lord at all times. His praise shall continually be in my mouth."

Battles vs. Wars

Our sons need to learn the difference between battles and wars. Sometimes it's better to walk away and lose the battle to be around tomorrow for the war.

There was a championship high school basketball game. One team had a star player who averaged more than 30 points per game. But the opposing coach knew the star player had a chip on his shoulder and did not know how to manage his anger. So he sent in one of his scrubs, one of his worst players. The player was told to foul the star player hard when he drove in for a lay up. This was in the very first quarter of the game. The star player was fouled hard, but because he had never been taught the distinction between a battle and a war, he hit the other player. Both players were ejected. While the second team only lost a player who had never scored a point, the team with the angry star player lost a potential 30 points—all because the boy did not know how to manage his anger.

The movie *Ragtime,* which you should watch with your son, has a powerful scene where Howard Rollins does not make the distinction between a battle and a war. The White community has been messing with him and they messed with his car. He made a car the war. He tried to fight his adversaries and was killed. His children lost their daddy and the wife lost her husband because Rollins made his car a war.

Battles are short term; wars are long term. Battles are fought for something you want; wars are fought for something you need.

Many of our boys have to have the last word. They make saying the last word the war when it should be the battle. They need to be taught that sometimes it is better to leave the battle, to let an adult have the last word, and to just be quiet. They'll win another day, but today was not their day. This is an important lesson our boys need to learn.

They need to learn anger management and the distinction between battles and wars. They need to take the chip off their shoulder.

In the next chapter these lessons will become more significant as we look at racial profiling and Africentricity.

Chapter 24: Africentricity/Racial Profiling

Life is not fair, and our sons need to know that. Life definitely is not fair if you're African American, an African American *male*, and a *poor* African American male.

Our children need to learn how to respond in situations where life is not fair. For example, your son is in class and he has raised his hand numerous times to be called upon by the teacher. The teacher ignores him. How does he respond? We've mentioned how important it is to maintain your son's spirit, the glow in his eye, his innocence, his enthusiasm, his desire to learn, his feeling that he can do whatever he wants in life, that he can be successful. If a parent is not cognizant that her son is being ignored in the classroom, his spirit could be broken without her ever being aware.

Parents, it is imperative that you visit your son's classroom. Ask your son if he has any concerns in class. Is the teacher calling on him to his satisfaction? Schools respond differently to students when they see parents actively involved in their sons' lives.

Here's another scenario. Two boys get into a fight at school. One boy is Black, the other is White. The White student is warned; the Black student is suspended for three days. How do you reconcile this with your son? Do you accept this? Are you willing to meet with the principal? Are you willing to meet with the PTA, the school board, the other student's parents? This kind of discrimination takes place every day, nationwide.

Russell Skiba's excellent research, "The Color of Discipline," indicates that for a White male to be suspended requires bloodshed or visibility of a knife or gun. African American males, however, may be suspended because of the way they look at a teacher, the way they walk, the way they shrug their shoulders. When White males are suspended, the reasons are very objective. African American males are victims of subjectivity.

We must prepare our boys for living in a racist country. There is tremendous fear of African American males. No population is targeted more than African American males. We have the greatest amount of melanin, which determines among other things, skin color. We live in a country controlled by White males. The greatest threat to White males is not females but other males. We saw this during slavery, the Tuskegee experiment, and today in prison populations. Our boys need to understand the environment in which they live.

Parents, have your sons read *The Autobiography of Malcolm X* and *The Autobiography of Jackie Robinson.* The racism many of our boys are experiencing is miniscule compared to the racism that was experienced by Jackie Robinson and Malcolm X.

Ask your son if he could have handled the sports career of Jackie Robinson. Have him close his eyes and imagine that he's up at bat. The White pitcher throws the ball, but wait, it's coming *at* him. The pitcher's trying to hit him! What would he do if, while running the bases, he gets spiked? After the game, his White teammates stay at a five-star hotel and eat at a nice restaurant while he must stay at a Negro hotel and eat at a Negro restaurant. How would he react? How do we teach our children to handle such situations?

Another excellent book is *The Autobiography of Nelson Mandela.* If our boys think they have it hard, they need to read about the life of Nelson Mandela. How would your son have handled being incarcerated for 27 years for a crime he did not commit?

Nelson Mandela did not allow the system to break his spirit. He decided to use the time to develop himself. He went from prisoner to president. Your son needs to have that kind of spirit. No one, no thing, no institution will break his spirit.

The best way to respond to racial profiling is to have an understanding of your history and culture. African American males play the race card too early. They play the wrong card. Many African Americans love telling me that there is a 300-point differential between Blacks and Whites on the SAT because the tests are culturally biased. That may be true.

What was Washington's first name? Europeans would say George. African Americans would say Harold or Booker T.

What color are bananas? Europeans would say yellow and green. African Americans would say brown.

The test could be biased, but why do Asians outperform Whites on a White test? Asians don't play the race card. They use their history and culture to *overcome* racism. We have not learned this lesson yet because we still perceive ourselves as *victims* of racism.

We not only play the race card too early, we play the wrong card.

The Jewish community was being discriminated against in Miami. They were not welcomed there by the White community. So what did the Jewish community do? Did they play the race card? Did they say the White man doesn't like me? Did they pack up and go home? Did they feel sorry for themselves?

Or did they buy the beach?

Asians study more than Whites and outperform them on a Eurocentric test. Jews pool their financial resources and buy a beach where they were once discriminated against.

African Americans not only play the race card too early but they play the wrong card. The cards we should play are the culture and history cards. Ask your son: if Black people are inferior, why do Whites discriminate? If we're inferior, then there's no need to discriminate. If we were lazy, why did they bring us to this country? They must know more about us than we know about ourselves.

The card Jews play is the culture card. Their motto is "never forget." Never forget your history and culture. If you do, you will always be a victim of racism.

It's unfortunate that many African American parents are dependent upon a Eurocentric school system to teach their children their history and culture. Few schools will teach your son that Imhotep, not Hippocrates, was the first doctor.

Few schools will teach your son that Ahmose, not Pythagoras, is the father of mathematics.

Few schools will teach your son that Africans built the pyramids in Egypt, and that Egypt is a country in Africa.

Frances Cress Welsing, in the powerful book *The Isis Papers,* makes a poignant point: until you understand White supremacy, everything else will confuse you. Our boys need to understand White supremacy. They need to view racism like a game of chess. They need to learn how to predict how the oppressors think. They need to understand the powerful quote by Frederick Douglass, "Power concedes nothing without a struggle."

We have taught our boys to play the race card too early and to play the wrong card. They are suffering from post-traumatic slavery disorder, and we must do everything we can to heal them and ourselves.

Before we left Africa, we considered ourselves African. When we went through the Door of No Return and got on the slave ship, we were told to call ourselves colored. Later on we became Negro, then Black, then Afro-American. Now we're almost back to where we began as African Americans.

Many of our people, and this could include your son, do not see themselves as African. This is another symptom of post-traumatic slavery disorder.

Does your son believe he's better in sports than in science? Better in music than math? Better in rap than reading? If he believes that being smart is acting White, your son is suffering from post-traumatic slavery disorder.

Does your son believe that good hair on females is long and straight? If he believes that the lighter you are, the prettier you are, he is suffering from post-traumatic slavery disorder.

Does your son believe that White lawyers, White doctors, White businesses, and White neighborhoods are better than African American lawyers, doctors, businesses, and neighborhoods? If so, your son is suffering from post-traumatic slavery disorder.

Your son's mental health is dependent on Africentricity—his history and culture. At some point, you and your son must visit Africa. If you can't take the actual trip there, watch movies like *Sankofa* and *Roots.* The only way to heal from a crime is to revisit the crime scene.

Your son must understand racism. Teach him the implications of DWB (Driving While Black) and SWB (Shopping While Black). Does he believe he can drive without taking lessons? Teach him his history and culture so that he will know which card to play and when to play it.

Your son and his three friends walk into a department store. If they walk in the store with book bags, if their jeans are going the wrong way, there's a good chance they will be profiled.

If they think they can go into the dressing room and not be watched by a video camera, they are sadly mistaken. They are asking for trouble. Your son needs to understand racism. Until he understands White supremacy, everything else will confuse him.

Your son must learn that he will be watched whenever he goes into a store. Don't get mad, get smart. Teach him how to turn the tables on this situation. Have him respectfully approach a store assistant or manager with the following empowering script:

> Good afternoon. My friends and I are going to spend a certain amount of money in your store today. If you want to watch us or follow us, you can. Better yet, we want to buy several different items, and rather than watching us as we walk around the store, why don't you just bring the items directly to us? We'll sit here and wait.

This is how wealthy people shop. Your son can change a negative shopping experience into first-class treatment. Rather than being watched and followed, they can make the store assistant run around and gather all the things they want to buy—as if they were the only customers in the store.

A second common type of racial profiling is DWB (Driving While Black). For some reason, if a Black male is driving, he is considered dangerous. If a young Black male is driving an expensive car, it couldn't possibly be his.

Have your son read *Yo, Little Brother. . .: Basic Rules of Survival for Young African-American Males* (volumes 1 and 2) by Anthony Davis and Jeffrey Jackson. The authors provide more than 200 strategies on how to address these issues.

Role play with your son before he drives anywhere. Remember, if you do not understand White supremacy, everything else will confuse you. Your son needs to know there's a good chance he will be pulled over by the police whenever he drives. Before my two sons drove, we played a game. I pretended to be the police, and they pretended to be driving a car. I pulled them over to see how they would respond.

I also taught my sons that before you get into anyone's car, check the car thoroughly because your homies may be setting you up. Check the glove compartment, under the seats, inside the trunk, and even under the hood. Your son doesn't need to be in a car with drugs or weapons. If a police officer finds them, everyone in the car becomes a suspect and an accomplice.

Does your son have a current driver's license?

Does your son have insurance?

Does everything work on the car?

Do you have a current license plate and city sticker?

Before playing the race card, make sure that everything that's required is in order.

Parents, teach your son how to behave if he is pulled over by the police. Is this a battle or a war? This is not the time to be macho and make a war. This is a battle, a battle that the police are going to win. Everything is in their favor. Your son needs to understand this. When the police pull him over:

- Do not get out of the car. Sit still and wait for the police to come to you.
- Understand that several police cars may arrive.
- Police will shine lights in your son's face.
- They may speak disrespectfully to your son.
- Your son needs to be on his best behavior.
- Your son needs to treat the officer(s) with respect: "Yes, sir" or "No, sir." "Yes, ma'am" or "No, ma'am."

- Your son should always keep both hands visible to the police.
- If they ask, show them your license and insurance card without any attitude.

Your son needs to understand that this story may not have a happy ending right away. He should secretly attempt to memorize the officer's name and badge number. The war will be won by you in the morning, not by your son tonight.

The prime time for police harassment of African American males is between 10:00 pm and 2:00 am. Your son should be in the house, not hanging out with his friends on the corner. Curfew times vary by city and day of the week. You and your son should know when he must come inside. Don't tempt the police.

There are speed traps where the speed limit can change from 40 mph to 30 mph in a block. Don't play the race card too early. Where's the racism in a change of speed limit? Your son needs to be taught to watch the signs and lower his driving speed. It's a speed trap, not a race track, so simply follow the rules of the road.

Your son should have a bond card. Insurance companies and AAA provide bond cards. Every Black male should have one and shouldn't leave home without it.

Let me share with you a horror story that happens too often in America. His name is Jerry Miller, and this incident occurred 25 years ago. Jerry Miller had just gotten off from work at a restaurant. The police stopped him and queried him. He worked about 100 blocks from where he lived. Seven days later, a White woman was raped in the neighborhood where Jerry Miller worked. Those police went straight to Jerry Miller's house. Because they had no suspects, they decided to pin the crime on Jerry Miller.

The police took Jerry Miller out of his house and questioned him for two days without letting his parents know where he was. They prosecuted him. The bond was $100,000. That means his family could have paid $10,000 to get him out on bail, but the family did not have enough money for the bond.

Before Blacks spend all their money on liquor, cars, jewelry, clothes, and everything else that depreciates almost instantaneously, it is imperative to have at least $10,000 in cash to provide, God forbid, bond for our sons.

Jerry Miller stayed in jail one year before trial. The White female victim could not identify him. She did not think Jerry Miller committed the crime. Two African Americans who worked for a city parking lot pinned it on Jerry Miller. There's a strong possibility that the police encouraged those city workers to do that.

Jerry Miller stayed in jail one year because his family could not post bond. It is difficult to develop a case when you are in jail for a year. Fortunately, the family did have enough money to hire an attorney, but that was not enough. Jerry Miller was convicted and sentenced to 45 years. He served 25 years, and only at the time of his release did the Innocence Project determine with DNA evidence that Jerry Miller did not commit the crime. He was exonerated and is no longer on the register list for sex offenders.

The reality is that Jerry Miller lost 25 years of his life. There are many reasons: racism, unfair judicial system, and the fact that his parents did not have money for the bond.

Compensation rates for wrongful imprisonment vary by state. Some states offer no compensation, and others offer less than $50,000 to compensate for a tragedy of this magnitude.

Your son needs to read *The Souls of Black Folk,* where W.E.B. DuBois describes our two warring souls. These souls are African and American. The million dollar question is, How do we remain Black and live in a racist country?

Our boys deserve better. They should be able to go into a store and not get hassled. Like White males, they should feel that police officers are their friends. Unfortunately, Black boys feel the police are their enemy.

Boys are victims of parents who have not developed any economic muscle. Our boys should be shopping at Black stores. Collectively we earn $723 billion, yet we spend only 3 percent of our money with each other. Why is that?

We play the race card too early, and we play the wrong card. The card we should be playing is the self-love card. We should all be spending at least 10 percent of our money with each other.

We need to use our political muscle, too. Politicians cannot win without the Black vote. How can we continue to allow a police department to police itself? Whenever there is a police infraction, the police review board reviews the case. This is ludicrous. Only an independent review board should be allowed to review police infractions. Until we make corrections on a political and economic level, DWB and SWB, unfortunately, will continue.

In the next chapter, we will look at the college and career development of Black males. Parents, if you have done your job well during the first 18 years, then rejoice. Your son will be going off to college to study and prepare for his career and the rest of his life.

Chapter 25: College and Career Development

This chapter could be a book by itself. If you are serious about ensuring that your son matriculates through college, I encourage you to read my book *Black College Student Survival Guide.*

Other excellent books on this subject are Michael Cuyjet's *African American Men in College* and *Helping African American Men Succeed in College* and the work of Freeman Hrabowski, *Beating the Odds: Raising Academically Successful African American Males.*

Does your son know he's going to college? Expectations are extremely important. Our sons need to rise to our high expectations rather than settle for our low expectations.

If you begin to talk about college during your son's senior year in high school, that's too late. You need to talk about your expectation that he will be going to college as early as possible. I know of parents who have their toddlers wear college sweatshirts and put college banners in their bedroom. That's how early the discussions need to begin.

It's disturbing to speak to high school seniors in, say, their second semester, and they still haven't taken the ACT or SAT. Many universities have already selected their freshmen students for the coming year. This places our students far behind in the college entrance game.

We play the race card too early, and we play the wrong card.

Parents, take your children on field trips to colleges. On weekends, take your children to every college within a 50-mile radius of your home. During spring breaks and summer vacations, take them to colleges around the country.

Every Black male should visit Morehouse. It is the only African American male college in America. I've had the privilege of speaking there almost every year. It is a tremendous honor to see thousands of African American males come together on one college campus with the sole mission of academically preparing themselves for their future.

The selection of which college to attend requires a great degree of thought. Not all colleges are the same. Listed below are the various types of colleges:

- Large colleges—10,000 students and greater
- Smaller colleges—10,000 students and fewer
- White colleges—90 percent White
- Black colleges—90 percent African American
- Urban colleges
- Rural colleges

Your son could attend Southern University in Baton Rouge, which is the nation's largest Black college with more than 10,000 students. Fifty percent of the professors are African American. Every day of the week he would have interesting cultural experiences.

Or he could attend the University of Minnesota at Morris where there are, as of the last time I spoke there, only 17 African American students. These students' greatest challenges are getting a hair cut and finding a Black music station on the radio.

I am biased toward Black colleges. They only have 14 percent of African American college students, but they produce more than 30 percent of African American graduates, an exemplary accomplishment. Some schools will admit you; other schools will go beyond and help you to graduate.

Some racists claim that Black colleges have lower standards than White colleges. If that's true, how do we explain the fact that more than 75 percent of African American graduates of Black colleges go on to White universities for their graduate degrees?

Black colleges encourage their students to continue their educational experience beyond graduation. I've met many African Americans who were so depressed after graduating from a White university that they had no desire to go on to graduate school for additional degrees.

Because I speak at numerous colleges annually, I know that all is not well at Black colleges. Many are suffering financially. As a result, many students who would have loved to have attended a Black college were not provided with the financial aid or scholarship needed to attend. They often end up at smaller White colleges, not because that's where they wanted to go but because the White college offered more financial aid.

In addition, some Black colleges are controlled by "Negro" leadership that refuses to keep pace with the times and needs of a new generation of students. This is the way we've always done it. Some college presidents have been in their posi- tions for more than 20 years, and few changes have been made.

I find many students taking their Black college experience for granted. For example, security must be provided at campus parties because of the problems cliques have with each other. The cliques—sororities and fraternities—divide Black students. There are even gang elements on some Black college campuses.

On the other hand, African American students at White colleges gravitate toward each other and help each other take advantage of the experience. A small but powerful network, they nurture and support one another.

The issue is not large or small, Black or White, urban or rural. The million dollar question is, Does your son want to go to college? Does he know he's going to college?

Is your son ready for college?

I distinguish between being in 13th grade and being a college freshman. Many students are in college simply because their parents wanted them to go. They had no other place to go. It's just another place to avoid reality.

Students who are in 13th grade still need their parents to discipline them. They need their parents to tell them to do their homework and help them study. They need their parents to help them with time management. Is your son in 13th grade or in college?

If your son is a college freshman, then he's self-disciplined. He understands time management. One reason why only 40 percent of African Americans graduate from college within five years is because of poor discipline and time management skills.

There are 168 hours in a week. Fifteen hours is an average course load. 168 – 15 = 153. Factor in 56 hours for sleeping (8x7), and that leaves 97 hours.

Students in 13th grade spend much of the 97 hours sleeping in their dorm room, hanging out in the cafeteria and student lounge, playing basketball—anything but studying. There should be a 2:1 ratio between study hours and class hours. If your son takes 15 hours (and many of our students are unable to maintain 15 hours), he should be studying a minimum of 30 hours. If he even smells probation, there should be a 3:1 ratio, or 45 hours of studying.

Africans from the continent and the islands have much better GPAs than Africans born in the U.S. The greater your *nia,* your purpose, the higher your GPA. When you understand why you are in college, that you came to America to become a doctor and return home to improve the living conditions of your home country, you are motivated to maintain a high GPA.

Some boys don't understand why they're in college. If they are clear on their *nia,* their purpose, they will do well in school.

Let's say you gave birth to twins, a boy and a girl. They both score 1400 on the SAT. They both have a 3.0 GPA. They both attend a Black college. The daughter graduates with honors, and the son flunks out. In this scenario we cannot play the race card. It's a Black college. The "not qualified" card cannot be played because they both scored 1400 on the SAT and they both had a 3.0 GPA.

For some reason, there's a 10 percent differential between African American females and African American males graduating from college. Forty-five percent of African American females and only 35 percent of African American males graduate within five years. Does the race card explain this 10 percent differential? Or could it be the following:

Do females study more than males?

Do females attend class more than males?

Do females take better study notes than males?

Do females study vs. cram?

Are females willing to utilize a tutor?

Are females better organized than males?

Are females more disciplined?

Are females more focused?
Are females more responsible?
Do females party less?
Do females date less?
Do females spend less time in the student lounge and cafeteria?
Do females get high less?
Do females spend less time at sports?

Dealing with our sons on these issues will increase the number of African American males who are admitted into college and their graduation rate.

Does your son know he can't return home after flunking out of college? The worst that can happen to him, flunking out, may not be a bad thing from his perspective. If he flunks out of college, he can return home and stay with his mother.

Mothers who have low expectations for their sons allow them to return home after flunking out. These mothers think their sons are doing well if they are taking three to six hours of coursework at a junior college and working ten hours at a food chain. They think that is significant. Six hours of college courses and ten hours working at a food chain. We need to raise our expectations.

If your son was involved in different positive activities growing up, he shouldn't have too much trouble choosing a major. This is an important decision. Unfortunately, many boys cannot give a different career for each letter of the alphabet. We need to expand our sons' career horizons. Mentoring is an excellent way for your son to learn about his many career options. If he never met an engineer, it would be difficult to consider engineering as a career. He wouldn't know about the many different types of engineers either.

Our sons should not choose a major and career purely based on income. I call that high-class prostitution. He will spend the next 40 years of his life possibly doing something he doesn't enjoy if he does it solely for money. Isn't that similar to what a prostitute does?

Many adults live for TGIF; they live for the weekends, vacations, and retirement. That's not God's best. Have your son memorize Jeremiah 29:11. God has a plan for your son's life, and it's not something he would hate Monday through Friday. It's something he will enjoy for the rest of his life.

There's a distinction between a job and a career. A career is something you love so much you'd be willing to do it for free. Our sons deserve careers and businesses, not jobs they despise.

College Financing

Unfortunately, college costs have gone up tremendously over the years. A financial aid package used to consist more of grants than loans. Today, parents and students are taking out more loans than ever before. Amazingly, students take longer to graduate when they have a loan package. If I were in school today and was accruing $10,000 to $20,000 per year in loans, it would not take me seven years to graduate. I would do everything I could to graduate in three or four years if for no other reason than to minimize the debt.

Parents, open a mutual fund for your son on his first birthday. You can open a mutual fund for as little as $50. No matter your income level, you need to start somewhere. On every birthday, contribute whatever you can to the mutual fund. Have your son review the statements regularly. He needs to know that the mutual fund is for his college education. If he gets a scholarship, it can be used to finance his business or to purchase his house.

A child is not at risk because he's from a low-income or single-parent home. He's at risk when he doesn't have any goals. How great would it be if our boys knew they had a mutual fund designed for college, their business, or to purchase property, and they knew this early in the game.

Our boys need to be taught Rule 72. Seventy-two divided by the rate of return will determine the number of years it will take for your money to double. If you have $10,000 in a checking or savings account earning 2 percent interest, it will take 36 years for your money to double.

But if you have your money in a mutual fund that has averaged an increase of more than 12 percent annually over the past 50 years, $10,000 should double in 6 years.

Teach your son that there are consequences to his behavior. My parents set up a mutual fund for me, and my parents did not play. My father had high expectations, and my mother loved me unconditionally. The two made a very good pair. My father told me in no uncertain terms, "If you make a baby, all of the money in your mutual fund will go to take care of your child." That would make our boys think twice about becoming sexually active because you've given them something to lose.

Career Development

I once spoke at a suburban school district whose student body was approximately 20 percent Black. They brought me in because they wanted me to "fix the children." There was nothing wrong with the school from their perspective. They didn't feel the problem was their low expectations, Eurocentric curriculum, and left-brain lesson plans. They felt the problem was with Black youth. They wanted me to persuade their Black male students to value education and work hard.

I love working with youth because they are honest, they have little tact, and they say exactly how they feel. They say to me, "Get a good education for what? And work hard for whom?" These are two excellent questions.

If working hard was the solution, Black people would be running America. No one has worked harder than African Americans in this country. Working hard may not be the only solution for success. There's some old money in America; 1 percent of the population owns 48 percent of the wealth, and 10 percent owns 86 percent of the wealth. I don't believe they earned that money because of hard work and the bootstrap theory.

When you talk to children about getting a good education, they see many adults who have degrees and were laid off and underemployed. They see other people making far more money than they make. I have college classmates who earned their degree in education but did not use it. They found they could make more money driving a truck or a bus than becoming a classroom teacher.

We tell children to "work hard" and "get a good education," but do we tell them why? Here's what individuals with various levels of education can expect to make over a lifetime:

- High school drop out: $750,000 (if they can find a job)
- High school diploma: $1,100,000
- Bachelor's degrees: $2,100,000
- Master's degrees: $2,500,000
- Doctorate: $4,400,000

Initially, I sell the students on the importance of a good education and working hard by showing them this chart. Obviously, education pays.

The Interview

It is important for students to understand the importance of the job interview. When speaking to the interviewer, you must make good eye contact. Your pants can't be going the wrong way. You shouldn't wear earrings. Although you may be nervous, you shouldn't mumble or offer a weak handshake.

We must teach our sons how to handle the interview. The economy has changed from a manufacturing economy to an information economy. There is a good chance they will be working in an office.

The rumors are that females type better than males, have better communications skills, and work better with co-workers. Males need to address these issues.

In defense of our youth, if you're telling boys that the best reason for learning standard English is to get a good job from the White man downtown, here's what youth in the hip-hop movement have to say: "I don't want to work downtown for the White man. I would love to earn my money by going pro in the NBA, getting a rap contract, or by becoming the first drug dealer never to be caught." For many of our youth, this is the definition of Black economics. What they lack is the context of a financially strong community that supports its own members yet trades with other communities. To engage in trade, you have to know standard English, which is the global language of business. If you cannot speak the language, no one will understand you and you will not succeed. The ability to communicate with others is fundamental to success in business and in life.

I applaud the entrepreneurial drive of today's generation of youth. When you discuss career and business options with your son, offer the following tried and true ventures:

- Entrepreneurship
- Stock Market
- Real Estate

Entrepreneurship. In the classic book, *Rich Dad, Poor Dad,* poor dad had a good education. Poor dad told his son to get a good education and work hard, but few employees are multimillionaires. You have a greater chance at becoming rich as an entrepreneur or by investing in real estate or the stock market than by getting a good education and working hard as an employee.

I encourage you to expose your sons to The National Foundation of Teaching Entrepreneurship. I'm on their board. They have an excellent curriculum for young people.

Work with your son on developing his business plan. Every Black male needs to have a business plan.

Stock Market. If our boys can sell crack, they can surely sell stock. We need to teach our children the stock market and Rule 72. Buy them a pair of Nike shoes and some Nike stock. Once a month, have your son compare the value of the shoes to the value of the stock.

Real Estate. We must teach our children the principles of real estate. Every piece of land and every building are owned by someone. How unfortunate that the Black community owns so little.

Our boys love hanging on corners, and gangs love to fight over turf. If they value turf that much, help them acquire the house in foreclosure down the street. Instead of these young brothers wasting their time on the corner, after school they could be rehabbing that house, flipping it, selling it, and reinvesting the money into more properties.

Blue Collar Work

The debate between Booker T. Washington and W.E.B.. DuBois needs to stop. Both white-collar skills and blue-collar skills have their place. I value both. As a doctor, Cliff Huxtable in "The Cosby Show" couldn't fix anything around the house. It was funny in the show, but in real life our boys need to be taught the importance of plumbing, carpentry, and electricity, and they need to know how much these trades pay.

It is tragic to see construction projects going on in the heart of the Black community and very few African Americans working on those jobs. Even flaggers get $20 and $30 an hour. Our boys need to be taught the importance of blue-collar skills.

Sales

Since our boys love to sell, they need to know there are many other products to sell besides crack. If you can sell, you will never be unemployed.

For many of us, the sales experience has been a detrimental one because we sold products we didn't like or value. If you sell something you yourself use, it's easy to work in sales. I fly with many White males *without a college degree* who are making six-figure salaries in sales.

There are numerous career options for young males. To review, they are:

- Entrepreneurship
- Stock Market
- Real Estate
- White-Collar Skills
- Blue-Collar Skills
- Sales

In the next chapter we will look at one of the most important decisions of your son's life, and that's his personal relationship with a Savior who says, "I will never leave you nor forsake you."

Chapter 26: Spirituality

Without a doubt, this is the most important chapter of this book. The most important question your son will ever have to answer is, Do you have a personal relationship with Jesus Christ?

God made us all empty, and then He gave us free will. Have you ever wondered why men lead the country in suicide?

Have you ever wondered why men leave their families more than women do?

Show me a man who is not connected to God, and I'll show you a man with no power. Many men are powerless because they do not want to submit to the Manufacturer.

You can take your car to the shop for an oil change, for the tires to be rotated, and for other simple repairs. But if there is something seriously wrong with the car, the only place that truly understands the car is the dealership, the manufacturer.

Men can deceive themselves and go to the bowling alley, the bar, become a womanizer, buy new cars and clothes, but there would still be something missing because they have not taken themselves to the Manufacturer.

Two groups that have the greatest problem believing in Jesus are males and young people. In this chapter we will look at how we can help our sons gain a personal relationship with Jesus Christ. I would be remiss in a book titled *Raising Black Boys* if I did not address the most important aspect of child rearing, and that's for parents to expose their children to their Lord and Savior.

Parents, you need to meditate Acts 16:31: "Me and my household are saved." There are many reasons why males and young people have such a difficult time giving their lives to Christ. In my books *Adam, Where Are You?*, *Why Most Black Men Don't Go to Church,* and *Developing Strong Black Male Ministries*, we go into far more detail than I can do in this one chapter.

In *Adam, Where Are You?* we list 21 reasons why Adam, i.e., most men, do not go to church. Not only do we have a problem getting Adam, Sr., to attend, we also have a problem getting Adam, Jr., to attend.

I speak at many churches for Youth Day. I look at the choir of 50 young people and there are 40 or so females and only 5 to 10 males. I understand why Adam, Sr., is not in church. As an adult, he makes his own decisions. But why isn't Adam, Jr., in church? Could it be that mothers give their sons the option of going to church? Some mothers make their daughters go but not their sons. The same mothers are distraught and disappointed that they have not been able to find a saved Black man, yet look at what they're allowing with their sons.

We make our children go to school, but we don't make them go to church. At first I was going to write that we make our children go to sleep, but there are parents who allow their sons to watch HBO and Showtime until the wee hours of the morning. I wanted to say that we make our children eat broccoli and Brussels sprouts, but that's not true either. Many parents who want to be buddy buddy with their children make eating vegetables optional. There are parents who give their children the option of attending mentoring and rites of passage programs. It is true that many parents are giving their sons numerous options. They have relinquished the responsibility of being parents.

Again I ask the question, why do you make your daughters go to church and not your sons?

Are you raising an atheist or agnostic in your house?

We could reduce crime in our neighborhoods if we induced Black males to be saved. How unfortunate that the group causing the greatest havoc in our community, 12-to-19-year-old males, are least represented in church.

We play the race card too early, and we play it wrong. We can't blame our problems on the White man. As parents, we make these decisions. I am so glad my parents taught me that even if I was going to party all night on Saturday, I would still be praising God all Sunday morning. If I was going to eat mama's greens, I had to praise mama's God.

I am so grateful that my parents raised me in the love and admonition of the Lord. They have gone on to be with the Lord, and I am happy for them. No more pain, no more sickness for them. It would be challenging to live in this world without my parents and not have a personal relationship with God. My parents knew that at some point they would no longer be with me physically, and you need to know that at some point you will not be able to raise your son and take care of him. Your son needs to know God for himself.

Is there prayer in your house? You've heard, "The family that prays together stays together." Does your family pray together before you leave to go to work and school?

Does your family pray together before you go to bed at night?

Does your family pray together over meals?

Does your son pray over his food at school?

Do your son's classmates know he's saved?

It's a sad commentary when you've given your life to Christ and no one knows. Is your son too embarrassed to give God the glory for his meal in the lunchroom cafeteria?

In 1962, prayer was taken out of schools. The next year SAT scores declined, and for the very first time, teen pregnancies increased. How unfortunate that we've taken prayer and scripture out of school and replaced it with security guards and metal detectors. And that's still not enough.

The good news, however, is that if your son knows the Lord for himself, if he has been taught the value of prayer, then the school did not take prayer out of school. Your son can pray to God whenever he wants.

Have you taught your son the power of the Word?

How many scriptures does your son know?

The first book your son should be exposed to is the Bible. How beautiful it would be if our sons knew the scriptures: "Thy word is hidden in my heart so I would not sin against thee" (Psalms 119:11) and "If you love Me, keep My commandments" (John 14:15).

Do you have Bible study in your house?

Have you taught your son the Trinity: Father, Son, and Holy Spirit?

Does your son know that the Greater One lives within him?

Does your son know that the Holy Spirit will teach him all things and bring all things to his remembrance?

Does your son know that when he's stuck on a particular question on an exam, he can ask the Holy Spirit for the answer?

I am concerned about families that celebrate Christmas but do not bring Jesus to the party. We now live in a culture where the Christ in Christmas has been replaced with an X (Xmas).

Let's make it personal. It's your birthday. There's plenty of food and drink. Everyone is invited to your party—but you. How would you feel? Well that's how Jesus feels when you celebrate December 25th and do not invite Him to the party. Families go deep in debt to buy their sons the latest video games at $150 a shot, but there's no mention that we're celebrating the birth of Christ.

When my sons were growing up, before the first gift was opened, our Bibles were opened, and we read about the birth of Jesus Christ. We thanked Him for being Lord, and then we opened the gifts.

Young males do not attend church for many reasons. The 85,000 churches in Black America can be categorized as follows:

- Entertainment
- Containment
- Liberation
- Graduate

Entertainment Churches. These churches are only open on Sunday from 11:00 am to 1:00 pm. They love to shout, holler, and hoop, but there's very little fruit that you can see in their ministries.

Containment Churches. These churches are also only open on Sunday from 11:00 am to 1:00 pm. Containment churches want you to give them all of your money without any explanation of how the money is going to be spent. The biggest wealth transfer in the Black community is on Monday morning, when Black churches deposit most of the $3 billion collected during Sunday services into White banks.

Entertainment and containment churches allow liquor stores and crack houses to be their neighbors. That explains why there can be many churches on a block but the neighborhood hasn't improved. These churches primarily attract elders and women.

Liberation Churches. These churches are open seven days a week. They adhere to a social justice ministry. The civil rights movement had its genesis in liberation churches. These churches make a difference in their communities. For example, Rev. James Meeks, pastor of Salem Baptist Church in Chicago, refused to allow liquor stores to be his neighbors. That neighborhood was voted dry. The Azusa ministry in Boston, pastored by Rev. Eugene Rivers, patrols the streets and makes it difficult for gang members and drug dealers to continue their criminal activities.

Liberation churches attract a greater percentage of men and young people than entertainment and containment churches. There are three churches I would love for you to visit:

Allen A.M.E., pastored by Rev. Floyd Flake in Queens, New York, has a youth church called Shekinah. If children truly are the future, then churches should be allocating a significant portion of their budget to youth ministries. At Shekinah, there is a separate sanctuary and youth pastor for young members. They are doing tremendous ministry as they empower their youth.

In your church, what percentage of the space is allocated for young people? What percentage of the ministry budget is allocated for young people?

The same applies to the Soul Factory, pastored by Deron Cloud, who has several churches in the Washington, DC-Maryland area. They are doing tremendous work with young people, especially low income.

The Haughville Church outside of Indianapolis has an excellent program called Hip Hop Haven, where young people can come in on Saturday night and enjoy gospel rap, clean videos, roller skating, board games, and pizza parties. They sleep over and wake up the next morning for a good breakfast before going into the sanctuary for a Sunday morning 8:00 am service.

We need more churches like Allen A.M.E.., Soul Factory, and Haughville to really value young people. Many parents make the mistake of thinking that all churches are the same. My wife and I travel more than 40 miles from our house to our church because we understand that not all churches are the same. It's amazing how we travel 20 or 30 miles to work and will even relocate from one city to another, but we don't put in the travel time to get to a church that meets our spiritual needs.

Graduate Churches. These churches develop babes in Christ to be mature saints. Many churches are filled with carnal Christians. The spirit is saved, but the flesh is still wild. They do not have a renewed mind.

Graduate churches believe that church should be viewed as school. My church is Living Word Christian Center, pastored by Bill Winston. Pastor Winston requires that everyone take foundation classes.

If you think two hours on Sunday will be enough to renew your mind against Satan, you are sadly mistaken. The real struggle is between the flesh and the spirit, with the mind regulating between them. Unfortunately, many Christians have minds that are not renewed. This explains why, on the low side, only 4 percent of Christians are tithers and on the high side, only 26 percent.

There is too much sickness, debt, and sin in the church. The divorce rate among Christians is as high as the world's. This is why men and young people are critical of the church.

They don't see any difference between church members and other people in the world.

Which type of church do you attend? To help your son reach his full potential, consider attending a liberation or graduate church. **Seventy percent of boys who were raised in church do not return to church as adults.** I believe it's because they were in entertainment and containment churches.

Sometimes it is hard to bring our sons to the Lord because they have to endure so much on the streets, and the church appears weak and passive. Many churches have a weak, blue-eyed image of Jesus Christ on the window pane, the hand fans, the Sunday school books, and the Cross. Males are visual, and images are extremely important to them.

Many elders would ask, what difference does it make if we are to worship Him in spirit and in truth? But elders, you can't have it both ways. If we're going to worship Him in spirit and in truth, there should be no images in our sanctuaries. If we're going to have images, then let's use Revelation 1:14–15 and Daniel 7:9 as our guides. They clearly point out that Jesus had hair the texture of wool, feet the color of bronze, and He came from the line of David, who was Hamitic. When Herod came looking for Jesus, Joseph hid his son in Egypt. You could not hide a White boy in Egypt, which is in Africa. Our boys need to know that.

They also need to know that there's no conflict in being both Africentric and Christocentric. It amazes me how people think that just because I have an African name I'm Muslim. The assumption is that you cannot be both Africentric and Christocentric. The reality is that the Garden of Eden story is an African story. The Pishon River is the White Nile; the Gihon River is the Blue Nile.

Moses was an African (Exodus 2:19), and Paul was an African (Acts 21:38).

Our boys need to know that most of the 265 slave revolts were led by Christian ministers. Nat Turner was a Christian. Gabriel Prosser was a Christian. Henry Harland Garnett was a Christian. Harriet Tubman was a Christian. Marcus Garvey was a Christian.

We need to revisit some biblical stories with our youth. One of my favorites is that of David killing Goliath with nothing more than a rock. When our boys are faced with the Goliaths in their neighborhoods, they need to know how David defeated his enemy. David didn't pray over Goliath. He threw something at him—in the strength of the Lord.

Peter was Jesus' right-hand man, and he was packing a sword, and he knew how to use it. He cut someone's ear off. I'm in no way encouraging violence, but our boys need to know that being a Christian doesn't mean you are weak on defense. Just try to rob a church, and watch how quickly security will respond. They won't respond with prayer and the Word; they will respond with force.

When Jesus saw money being exchanged in the sanctuary, He didn't ask his disciples to escort the vendors out. Jesus overturned the money tables and put those vendors out of the temple. Our boys need to understand that there's no inconsistency in having a strong relationship with the Lord and knowing self-defense and martial arts.

Unfortunately, many of our boys have been raised in entertainment and containment churches. They need to be exposed to liberation and graduation churches. Seventy percent of males who were required to attend church as boys do not return when they become adults. Many believe they are saved since they were baptized at their mama's church when they were younger. They believe that is their insurance card. There's no need to go to church because they already have their reservation in heaven.

These men don't see church as school, where a renewing of the mind takes place. They don't see any difference between those in church and those outside of church. They logically think that instead of going to church, they'll keep their money and their time and do what they need to do to develop themselves in the world. Since there's no difference between Christians and those in the world, why not?

Males often say, "I'm a good person." They've seen the pastor sleep with other women. The deacons are cheating.

Christians in the church are doing all kinds of things, and the non-churchgoer is not doing any of that. Such a man believes that since God is a good God, there's no way He would allow the sinning pastors and deacons to go to heaven and not give him the same privilege. These are the men who are involved in Cub Scouts, Boys Scouts, and Little League baseball. They're doing things to clean up the neighborhood.

The reality is that just because you got baptized at 7 does not mean you're going to heaven. scripture says, "Depart from me, I never knew you" (Matthew 7:23). The Bible does not say, "Once saved, always saved." Nowhere does it say, "Because of your good works you are going to heaven."

The gospel is not based on good works. scripture clearly says, "Your righteousness is filthy rags" (Isaiah 64:6). You don't go to heaven because you did good things on earth. You go to heaven because you have submitted to God through Jesus Christ. This is why so many men have a difficult problem submitting to the Manufacturer. But no one knows you better than your Manufacturer.

Parents, expose your son to the following scriptures that are taught in graduate churches:

- Joshua 1:5-8
- Numbers 13:30
- Proverbs 18:21
- Matthew 6:33
- Matthew 9:27–30
- Matthew 18:18
- Mark 9:23
- Mark 11:23–24
- John 14
- John 15:5
- Philippians 4:13
- 1 Timothy 2–15
- Hebrews 11:5
- 1 John 5:14
- 3 John 2

These are power scriptures, and your son needs to know them.

In the next chapter we will look at why "it takes a village."

Chapter 27: It Takes a Village

Once there was an African community where a herd of young male elephants were killing each other. The decision makers thought about killing these young elephants, but a wise elder realized that they were not to blame. The problem had developed because there were no adult male elephants in the herd. So they sent the young male elephants to another part of Africa where adult male elephants resided. In less than a month, their destructive behavior had ceased.

What we see in the animal kingdom we also see among humans. The problem has never been with our boys. Our boys need men in their lives. **Every boy needs a male role model.**

Between infancy and 6 years old, boys gravitate to their mothers. Although they watch what their fathers do as young as 6 months old, the mother is dominant in the earliest years of a young boy's life.

Between the ages of 7 and 11, boys begin to identify with their fathers. They want to shave and wear their fathers' clothes. They want to go where their fathers go.

At the age of 12 and beyond, every boy needs a mentor. The years from 12 to 18 are critical. Decisions about college and choosing a major are made during these years.

Ideally, a boy's mentor should be his father. Whether it's the father or not, every boy needs a respected male figure to learn from.

I believe in the power of mentoring and rites of passage programs. However, there are differences between the two. Listed below are the reasons why I favor rites of passage.

Mentoring	Rites of Passage
No curriculum	A curriculum
Individualistic	Collective

Rites of passage programs have a curriculum, most of which includes lessons on African history and culture. They teach the Nguzo Saba and Ma'at. They teach career development, politics, economics, and physical development.

In rites of passage programs, the men work together. A powerful group experience, these programs transcend the individual. Having a group of men work together helps with consistency. If one or two men are absent, the program goes on. The program is not dependent on individuals.

On the other hand, mentoring programs are totally dependent on the mentor. If the mentor is absent, there is no meeting that day. Your son could be a Christian and be mentored by an atheist or agnostic. Your son could be mentored by someone who is Eurocentric, who has values like Clarence Thomas and Ward Connerly. Your son could be mentored by someone who is gay.

I encourage parents to place their sons in a rites of passage program. If that's not available, make sure you interview the mentor before your son establishes a relationship with him. Make sure the mentor reflects your values. After each meeting, review with your son what he discussed with his mentor.

It takes a whole village to raise a child, and that is not a cliché. If you think you can raise your son by yourself, you are sadly mistaken.

There are two types of parents in America: givers and takers. Takers want you to pick up their sons and drop them off. They say they value your program, but not to the extent that they would be willing to drop off and pick up their own child. They say they value your program, but they never offer to volunteer or contribute in any way. These parents want you to expand the program to every day of the week. They wouldn't mind if their sons spent the night with the mentor or rites of passage leader.

Takers let their sons decide whether or not to participate in the program. If you gave your son the option of playing basketball or enrolling in a rites of passage program, which would he choose? Between hanging out or going to a rites of passage class, which would he choose? Between watching television or going to a rites of passage class, which would he choose? Ironically, the sons of takers need these programs the most, but the parents do not require their attendance. As their sons become older, takers allow more options. These parents are involved less and less in their sons' lives.

Givers are exactly the opposite. I've worked in many mentoring and rites of passage programs, and I just love working with givers. They believe in the law of reciprocity. They see how much the men are giving to their sons, and they are appreciative. They show their appreciation by first making sure their children are present every week. They drop them off and pick them up on time.

I love it when they offer to volunteer by providing supplies, food, transportation for field trips, financial donations, and great ideas; and they encourage the leaders.

Which type of parent are you?

It takes a village to raise a child because parents cannot be in all places at all times. Even my parents couldn't watch me all the time. That's why the village is so important. Once, when I was a freshman in high school, we got out early because we had a half day of school. Everyone knew it was a half day except two key people in my life: my mother and father. I had it all planned. My girlfriend and I were going to have sex that afternoon. We were halfway up the steps of my house when my next door neighbor stuck her nosey head out of the window and questioned what I was about to do.

It takes a whole village to raise a child. Parents, teachers, and neighbors need to be on the same side. Unfortunately, many parents who are insecure do not like other adults giving their children direction. Also, many adults are afraid of children, so they do not give direction. Youth admit that they often act the way they do because adults let them.

On the other hand, adults have told me they sometimes chastise youth on the street, the bus, and in other public settings, and the youth responded positively. If my next door neighbor had been silent and not said anything to me, my girlfriend could have gotten pregnant as a result of that act. My whole career, my life, would have changed. We must reduce, if not eliminate, any idle time that our children have after school and weekends.

Youth want to know where they are supposed to go. If not on the corner, then where? Where are the programs? It has gotten so bad that some malls are not allowing teenagers to enter after a certain hour without an adult.

Did you know that some Cub Scouts, Boy Scouts, and Little League teams are being run by women? It is not that women want to be scout leaders. Mothers don't really want to coach Pee Wee and Little League baseball. However, they do want their sons in constructive programs and off the streets.

The million dollar question is, Are men so self-centered that they cannot volunteer their time to give some direction to our boys? Only 32 percent of our children have their fathers in the home. Is the village strong enough to raise the other 68 percent?

I appeal to every man reading this book to volunteer a minimum of two hours per week to their local schools, churches, mentoring program, rites of passage program, Cub Scouts, Boy Scouts, Little League baseball—whatever youth activities boys are involved in.

Sometimes mothers tell me they don't know where the programs are. Listed below are program resources you should contact.

- Your local church
- Park district
- Local school
- Colleges
- 100 Black Men
- Fraternities
- Black Men and Boys National Resource Center
- 21st Century Foundation

In every city there are programs available for your son. In fact, many of those programs are underutilized, especially by adolescents. It is so frustrating for men who work in these programs. These programs are free, and they are excellent. But they are dependent on parents mandating their sons' attendance.

Some of the programs try to sweeten the deal with basketball, food, and video games. Still, it is so unfortunate that these programs have to market themselves to 12-to-18-year-old males who are allowed to make the final decision on whether or not to attend.

Our boys play enough basketball. Parents, it is not too much to ask that your sons be required to spend time with positive men who want to teach them history, culture, economics, politics, career development, and other subjects in rites of passage programs.

If we are not willing to do everything I've described in this book, our boys will suffer. The next chapter looks at how to help boys who have failed to reach their full potential.

Chapter 28: Alternatives

I pray that this chapter does not pertain to you. I hope it never reaches this point. I receive too many letters and phone calls from parents, mostly mothers, who have thrown up their hands because they do not know what to do about their sons. The son has dropped out of school, does not want to go to school, has been expelled from school, does not want to go to college, does not want to work or do anything around the house. It appears that the only thing he wants to do is lay up in his mama's house, disrespect her, listen to rap music, and stay out late. He may be involved in a gang and drugs.

There are two sons. The parents had one child when they were 19 and the other when they were 29. One graduated from college, and one is a prison inmate. Were they raised the same? Were they given the same amount of time? Did they each receive the same amount of advice and wisdom? Were they each given the same resources? Was one child favored over the other?

When I tell this story, I often ask parents if the two boys were, indeed, raised the same? Sometimes they answer too quickly. Let me share some good news from Pastor I.V. Hilliard at New Life Christian Center in Houston, Texas. His story is that one of his children messed up. Pastor Hilliard was asked how he felt. He said, "I didn't mess up. I'm not ashamed. They messed up. God gives all of our children free will, and neither He nor parents can violate our sons' free will."

If you can honestly say that you provided the best parenting program for your son and he refused to take advantage of those experiences and wisdom, then his failure is not on you. You do not need to take that guilt to the grave. You did the best you could with your son.

If our sons have gotten into trouble, we need to ask ourselves, what are the alternatives? Where is he going to live?

Living Arrangements. Many parents, especially mothers, believe their sons should stay in the house because the streets are so dangerous. He's 40 years old, still lying around the house, still watching videos, and he's resentful when you ask him to do anything, including helping you bring in the groceries that he's going to eat. Some parents feel it's still better for him to stay at home than go out into that mean, cold world.

Parents, make it clear that your son cannot stay at home. If he must stay at home, however, you'll need to change your relationship from parent-son to landlord-tenant. As landlord, you will require the following:

1. He will have to pay rent, plus utilities and food.
2. He will have to do his percentage of the chores.
3. He will have to be a full-time student and work a minimum of 20 hours per week.
4. The lease is for one year, and it will be reviewed on an annual basis.

Parents, especially mothers, do you have the strength, the fortitude to demand this arrangement? He can no longer pimp off his mother. He now has to be a responsible tenant. He needs to become a man.

Another option is for you to identify other parents who are in a similar situation. The boys could rent space in your home, or rather than living in your house, they could live together in their own apartment.

Field Trips. Take your son on field trips to the morgue, an inner city funeral home on a Saturday, the emergency room of a public hospital at midnight on a Saturday night, and to a drug abuse program where he can observe a baby born on cocaine trying to withdraw. He needs to go to a local jail. In fact, if you can have your son placed in a jail temporarily in a secure environment where he's not involved with other inmates, that would be ideal. He should watch the documentaries "Scared Straight" and "Lock Down."

Crisis Mentoring. Also, your son should spend a day or several days with the most respected man you know. I encourage you to pay this man. His job is to advise your son on some of the things he did not do during his first 18 years. This will be money well spent. Make sure this is the man you respect the most, someone you have total admiration for—not a man you just happen to know.

Counseling. Your son needs professional counseling. Again, this will be money well spent. He needs counseling on career development, academics, financial planning, what it means to be a man, a husband, and a father.

Have your son sit down with your pastor or a minister. Your son needs to get to the root of the problem: it is spiritual. I pray that you have a pastor, and hopefully he leads a liberation or graduate church.

Boot Camp. Create your own boot camp. This intensive boot camp would consist of martial arts, African history, tutoring, chores, and an internship. The camp would last for 1 to 12 months. I recommend that you create the boot camp because the next option is to send your son to a real boot camp. My concern is that because we live in a racist country, your son may not receive just treatment. I've heard horror stories about the treatment some African American males have had to endure at boot camps. If you must send your child to a boot camp, make sure you solicit references. Also, visit the camp before you send your son.

Boarding School. You can send your son to a boarding school. One of the best is Piney Woods in Mississippi. Ideally, we need more boarding schools, but they are not cheap. They can run from $10,000 to $20,000 and up per year. Because we have so few boarding schools, even they have become selective with their admissions. Unfortunately, your son may not qualify for Piney Woods if he is in deep trouble. Visit the school's website for further information, as well as sites for other schools in your area.

Amer-I-Can. The Amer-I-Can program founded by Jim Brown is doing excellent work turning around gang members, drug dealers, and others who have lost their sense of direction. This is another program for you to consider.

Back to Nature. Many of our youth simply need a different environment outside of urban areas. I encourage you to contact the Shrine of the Black Madonna. They acquired land in South Carolina. Any organization or church that has acquired land in the country would be a good place to send your son so that he can clear his head and regain focus on what he wants to do with his life.

The Military. It amazes me how God can give us our sons for 18 years and we fail to teach them to make their bed, do their chores, and do well academically. Yet they can go to the military and in six weeks of boot camp they now know how to get up early and do all these things.

The tragedy is that you can't just send your child to the military for boot camp. It requires a three-to-four-year commitment. American politicians are trigger happy. They love to send other people's children to war, and our sons are always on the front lines of dangerous, bloody wars. You can count on one hand and have several fingers left, the number of children of parents in the executive branch and Congress that are serving in the military.

If you must send your child to the military, make sure he receives a bonus for signing and an education. Make them put these benefits in writing. The military loves to promote and promise all the educational programs that are available, but they do not tell you that because of a soldier's responsibilities—six months in one part of the world and six months in another—there is little time to attend classes. Make sure your son signs up for the minimum contract. Make sure he doesn't reenlist.

My prayer is that you never have to read this chapter.

Epilogue

I've enjoyed writing this book for you. I have visualized you throughout. This book has made me revisit my childhood, rearing my sons, and now my grandparenting experience. I will be praying for you and your sons.

Always remember that your sons do not belong to you. They are children of God. Give your sons to the Lord, cast your cares upon Him, and let Him raise your sons.

To God be the glory!

References

1 U.S. Statistical Abstract, 2006

2. Ibid.

3. Hart, Betty, and Risley, Todd. *Meaningful Differences* (Baltimore: Brookes, 1995).

4. Lush, Jean. *Mothers and Sons* (Grand Rapids: Baker, 2001), pp. 117-120.

5. *Black Issues in Higher Education.* "Yale Study: African American Pre-K Students Twice As Likely to Be Expelled," June 2, 2005, p. 10.

6. *Education Week,* November 3, 1999. *Washington Post,* July 6, 2004.

7. Clay, Richard. *Raised Wrong—Educated Worse* (Detroit: NJIA, 2005), p. 86. Corbett, Augustus. *How Public Schools Fail Black Boys* (Arlington: Revival One, 2006), p. 24.

8. Johnson, Robert. *Strength for their Journey* (New York: Broadway, 2002), p. 202.

9. Ibid., p. 83.

10. *Journal of Pediatrics.* "Exposure to Degrading Versus Non-degrading Music Lyrics and Sexual Behavior Among Youth.," vol. 118, no. 2.

11. Biddulph, Steve. *Raising Boys* (Berkley: Celestial Arts, 1997), p. 170.

Notes

Notes

Notes

Notes

Notes

Notes

_____

_____

_____

_____

_____

_____

_____

_____

_____

_____

_____

_____

_____

_____

_____

Notes

Notes

Notes

Notes

Notes

Notes

_____

_____

_____

_____

_____

_____

_____

_____

_____

_____

_____

_____

_____

_____